JANUARY 6TH

JANUARY 6TH

JOHN SIZER

To order additional copies of this book, contact:
Xlibris
1-888-795-4274
www.Xlibris.com
Orders@Xlibris.com
811666

CONTENTS

CHAPTER 1

JANUARY 6

On this day, I discovered that I had sixteen $100 bills in my wallet. Every account that I thought I had was completely empty. I had resigned from my great teaching position and was not to be rehired. My wife of fifteen years—who had never had so much as a speeding ticket—was going to prison. The 4,800-square-foot home that I thought was paid for was in foreclosure. The two Cadillacs that I thought were also paid for were about to be repossessed. I had a twelve-year-old girl who had never known anything but a life of gymnastics, suburbs, nice schools, and elaborate vacations. Her life and mine were about to completely change. We both fully discovered on this day that all the things that her mother—my wife—had been telling us for months and years were nothing but lies. We discovered that she was a sociopath, liar, manipulator, and gambling addict all in one day. I had been a successful teacher and coach for nineteen years and lived in an affluent suburb of Shadowmont that is called Townsend. At that time, I taught in Townsend's school district—a huge district of nearly 18,000 students. I was coaching football at Saints Peter and Paul High School, a nationally prominent program. The life that my daughter, Amelia, and I had was about to do a complete 180.

We had been staying with relatives outside of Aldbridge for the holidays. At this time, I had resigned in order to cash out my state-teacher retirement to help my wife. My wife, Roseanne, had created an elaborate set of lies and documents that made me feel comfortable with this decision. We had taken in her very ill sister years before. Roseanne had created documents that stated that we had won a medical malpractice suit for nearly $500,000 and it would go to us—her caregivers. At the time, she explained that our accounts were frozen by Social Security. She made it out to have something to do with her ill sister and said she needed an attorney because all of these people were coming after her. After months of deliberation, I did what she asked. I took out my more than $200,000 retirement to help her. We hired an attorney and paid him several thousand dollars up front. We paid off people who were trying to sue her—an act that was like only putting a Band-Aid on a gusher, and we kept the last $80,000. We took this money with us to her family's house. During this Christmas "vacation," she was basically on the lam as there were warrants out for her arrest in two counties. She told us a web of lies; she said that this was all a mistake, and of course I believed her. My daughter was very involved in gymnastics at the time, and I wanted to get her back to Shadowmont so she could practice. Roseanne kept trying to drag out this stay and succeeded for a few days. Finally, I put my foot down and said Amelia and I were going back. I mentioned the $80,000, and she said it was probably safer to keep it in her cousin's gun case and she would bring it back with them for her upcoming court date in Shadowmont County on January 6. Amelia and I went home, and I would spend a few days working out by myself and taking Amelia to and from gymnastics. In the early morning of January 6, Rosanne and her cousin Mike arrived for her court date. We drove Rosanne to the courthouse and awaited her hearing. At this time, Mike, Amelia, and I still believed that this was just a huge mistake and everything would be fine. When her hearing started, a sheriff came over and informed me that they would be placing her in handcuffs immediately after it and then they would take her to another county for another proceeding. I remember saying "Good. Let's get this cleared up." They did just that. Roseanne was placed in handcuffs and led away. Her cousin Mike and I went back home and waited to hear from her. Mike and I were anxious as we stood around my marble kitchen island. The phone rang, and it was Roseanne. She said, "You need to bail me out."

I said, "OK. Where is the money?"

She said, "Call Tabitha." (She is one of our close friends, and she had stuck by us through this.)

I said, "Why would I call Tabitha when we have $80,000?"

She then proceeded to dodge various questions. Then Mike ran up from the basement with the small fireproof safe that we had carried the money in. I felt relieved and asked Mike where the key was. He told me that Roseanne had said that I had it. Roseanne had told me that Mike had it. Mike, being a mechanic, said he knew how to open it, and we went to the garage. Our home had a large three-car garage with a concrete floor. Mike said, "I will drop it on its corner, and it will pop right open." He did and it worked; out came the oversize lunch bag that we had placed the $80,000 in. I took the bag to the kitchen island. I said to Mike, "Wait till you see this." Not everyone has seen a cash amount this big. Mike was very excited! I tore open the bag and saw hundreds of sheets of notebook paper that were carefully folded over in letter-size shapes and wrapped with rubber bands. Mike told me later that he will never forget the look on my face at that moment.

I then realized that I had $1,600 to my name, no job and soon to have no house, no cars, and a twelve-year-old girl to take care of. The phone rang again, and I heard Roseanne's voice. "John, you need to get down here and bail me out now. It's only $1,500!"

I replied as tactfully as I could, "I wouldn't bail you out if it was fifty motherfucking cents because that'll buy a bag of ramen noodles for my daughter!" And then I hung up the phone.

I was suddenly flooded with the realization that she was guilty of every single thing that she was accused of and then some. I later found out that she had done much more and much worse to her blood relatives. Had her relatives chosen to press charges, she would have earned far more than five years in prison—five times that number, actually. I thought of having worked my heart out for nineteen years to save and build the life we had. I had a daily routine that involved waking up at 4:00 a.m. so I could study Quicken (a finance program) while taking my coffee. I would leave Roseanne notes of the bills we had to pay and the amounts we had to pay and forecast different accounts months and sometimes years ahead to see any potential bumps in the road. I had read dozens of finance books in order to have a great understanding of how to be debt-free and retire early if I so wished. We would have budget meetings monthly to make sure this plan was in place. She lied to my face for years, and I believed her.

I found myself crying for the next three mornings while leaning over that same kitchen island as my twelve-year-old girl ate breakfast. I spent those days not knowing what to do. I prayed hard to God for the strength to get Amelia to her high-school graduation. *Please let me get her to graduation. After that, I don't care what you do with me,* I thought. I spent those three days promising Amelia with tears running down my face that I would always take care of her.

What made me a strong-enough man to overcome this much adversity? Well, it all started at a young age.

CHAPTER 2

ELEMENTARY SCHOOL

The two biggest things about my childhood that I remember are the lake and football. My dad, his parents, and their parents were all from a small town near the lake. My earliest memories are the ones of me living in that town and taking advantage of the lake and everything to do with the lake. My grandfather bought me a Zebco fishing pole for my sixth birthday. A picture of the first time I used it was on the front page of the newspaper. My mom must have bought a hundred copies of that newspaper. She still mentions how the caption stated, "Fishing for fun in the sparkling sun." I could and would fish for hours whenever I had the chance. Fishing and swimming in the lake were my two biggest hobbies during the summer. There was a huge amusement park there, and it was where my mom worked. She worked there during the summer, and she had free access to the beach on her day off. Well, her day off turned into our day off. That's what we would call it, and it was always the best day of the week. I remember going to a convenience store with Mom and my two older sisters; we bought a Styrofoam cooler and loaded it up with lunch meat, snacks, and treats for the day. We would spend those days swimming, burying each other up to our necks in sand, and just having fun. I was always into sports, especially football. I would have my mom time me as I did just about anything. I would run from one end of the fence and back to the beach just to get a time. Then I would do it again and again in order to beat the previous time. We had all our best times as kids at the lake. During those early lake years, we lived in five different homes and in three different towns. You're going to have to pay a little bit of attention because we moved a lot. We moved so often, people always asked me if I was a military kid. Well, I sort of was. My dad served as a marine in Korea. He was also one of five children and the son of a prominent funeral-home owner. At nineteen, my dad "beat the draft," as he explains it, and went down to the recruiter and signed up to be a US Marine. My dad returned home to continue the funeral business. He was physically unharmed. His mental state was a different story. My uncles and cousins said that when he returned, he was not the same. The war had brought out a form of manic-depressive illness called seasonal bipolar disorder. With seasonal bipolar disorder, as the seasons changed, so would his highs and lows. When spring came, he would start to get "high," as we called it. This would begin the manic stage of his illness. During these times, he would make bad decisions that would cost him all kinds of things—mostly his jobs at various funeral homes. Then when fall rolled around and the weather got colder, he would become normal or acted like the dad that I loved. If you have ever been close to an unmedicated bipolar person, you would know the mania is extremely difficult for anyone to take. So in the end, you will find out that I was forced to move nine times before I was eighteen years old. I attended five different elementary schools, one junior high school, and four completely different high schools.

My first elementary school was a Catholic school. My dad would give us rides to school in some kind of Cadillac. It would be an old '70s hearse or limousine. Since then, I have always loved Cadillacs. Ironically, for some psychological reason, my sisters have always hated Cadillacs since then. Whenever it was financially possible, my dad would send us to Catholic schools. I went to that school for my kindergarten years up to the first two grades, and I enjoyed it as well as anything. The teachers and nuns, as you can imagine, were always nice to us, and I never did anything so wrong that I would deserve to be punished. We would walk to church during the week, and my dad would always take us again on Sunday. I later learned to not care at all for church. Nothing against God or anyone's belief in God. I just saw too much hypocrisy through the years and have always simply worked to be as good a person as I could be without having to sit through the sermons and listen to all the people who act so happy to see you. I saw a lot of it as fake.

In third grade, we moved to Wheatland, and I went to Rosewall Elementary. It is kind of odd now, looking back on it, because it was really only seven miles away from my former school. In Wheatland, we lived in a beach community that was also great because we only had to walk two blocks to reach a very nice beach. Our home was a two-bedroom cottage. The interior walls were made of cedarwood. Our bedroom doors were like shutters that folded open and shut. I remember that so distinctly because one winter, my grandparents came to visit us. My sisters and I stayed in a room that had a built-in bed and a set of bunk beds. Grandma was to sleep in the built-in one that night. When it was time for bed, my grandmother made sure we used the restroom first because she hated our dog and wanted to keep her out of the room. She tied pieces of cloth up and down these shutter-type doors to make sure that Baby, our dog at the time, stayed out. Well, nature called me in the middle of the night, and I couldn't untie these incredible knots. I had to wake up Grandma, and of course, she wasn't moving too quickly. She was very slow. I ran to the bathroom but didn't make it. At the time, it was the most horrific thing that could happen to an eight-year-old boy. I locked myself in the cedar bathroom with the cedar door. I cleaned everything as best as I could and deliberated as to what to do with the evidence. My master plan was to put my pajamas back on and tiptoe my way to the garage. We had a one-car garage with rafters. I flung my soiled underwear into those rafters and made my way back to the top bunk. I felt as if I had gotten away with murder and thought no one would ever know. No one did know until the next summer—when my parents decided to turn that one-car garage into a third bedroom. I remember my dad calling my name while he was up in those rafters. My sisters and mom had beaten me there, and there stood my dad with his left hand on the ladder, and in his right hand was a pen that dangled my six-month-old Popeye underwear. My sisters had a field day with that one!

We swam daily all summer long. This is also where I played my first organized sport: I played coach-pitch baseball for the Wheatland Lions Club. I still have the club shirt hanging in my bedroom now—forty years later. That year, the things that stood out at this school to me were mainly gym and recess. I loved to play anything and everything. I also loved to race anyone who wanted to. I wanted to be and tried to be the fastest kid in school. I loved to have fun and played whatever game was happening in the gym.

In fourth grade, I found myself living in Springfall. It's a peninsula out in the lake. Here we lived in a community known mainly for summer vacationers; it was a child's paradise. The street in this community of cottages was a dock as opposed to the beach we had in Wheatland. The great thing about it for a kid was there were parks, the dock, shuffleboard, basketball courts, horseshoes, roller-skating, sailboating, tennis, biking, a game room, a movie theater, and I could go on. It was a kid's paradise with an added bonus: New kids were coming every week. You met a new set of friends every week all summer long. Then once school started, I picked up where I left off in third grade. I loved gym and recess and pretty much did all my schoolwork. It was a great school. I attended Springfall School in fourth grade and half of fifth grade and had lived on the lake all my life to this point.

In the spring of 1981, President Reagan was shot. This was the first really big news event that I remember as a child. My dad always watched an excessive amount of news but never more than during that time. My entire family must have watched this a hundred times at least. It was surreal that anyone would do this to all of us kids, especially me being the youngest.

Then I remember my parents telling me we were moving. I had never minded before now because we always lived on the lake and it was never a big deal to me. We were going to a place that was an hour from the lake, and we were to live above a funeral home. Living above a funeral home didn't bother me because I had grown up in them. Not being near the lake was what I remember being upset about. The next day at school, we were using the pool for PE class, and I remember telling one of my friends that I had to move to Oldgrass and I was upset. My friend told me that one of our other friends moved there and they had a peewee football team. At that moment, my opinion about moving completely changed. I couldn't wait to move and start playing football because for as long as I could remember, that's all I wanted to do. I wanted to play football and eventually play football in the NFL. So early in my fifth-grade year, we moved to Oldgrass. I attended another Catholic elementary school. This was my first chance to play organized basketball. It was an interesting season; I fouled out of every single game and maybe scored a dozen points all season. I had fun there, and again, I loved recess. I remember coming in from recess; I was completely soaked with sweat during math class, and I lifted my shirt up to try and air myself out to my teacher's disgust. I vividly remember diving onto a blacktop to tag kids down in football. I was beyond excited to play baseball that summer and football in the fall. I got a job of delivering papers because I knew one had to buy their own equipment for football. I remember that I paid $35 for that first set of football pads. I still have the helmet hanging in my parent's garage today.

I was able to play football during my first year there and another year of basketball before we again needed to move during my sixth-grade year. We moved very far from the lake this time, and I was to attend a medium-sized country school outside of Dayton called Valwick. I got there just in time to play Little League baseball. This is the fifth elementary school that I attended. These moves were at times disappointing and at other times exciting. My mom always made me feel loved and tried to make everything seem OK. My dad was busy working or being fired from his jobs, and the current season determined how I felt about him. Life with a seasonal bipolar person is never easy for anyone. Regardless of the five moves, I loved my sports, recess, and gym class and managed to do solid with my academics. I learned at a young age to make the most of every situation, and sports always kept me focused.

CHAPTER 3

GRADES 7, 8, AND 9—VALWICK

We ended up living in Valwick the longest we ever lived anywhere. We moved there with enough time left in the school year that I could meet some kids and play Little League baseball that summer. My sixth-grade teacher, Mr. Fayford, ended up being my baseball coach. I had fun that summer. I played second base for the Spartans. I stole thirty-seven bases and loved to steal home. I would have stolen more if I could have hit better. When baseball finished, football camp started. I was extremely excited to go to the camp and learn from the high school players and coaches. I was extremely enthusiastic then when it came to this game, and I still am now. It was an interesting three years in a lot of different ways. Grades 7, 8, and 9 are awkward for any kid. They are especially awkward when you're the new kid and a very late bloomer with sisters that are four and five years older than you. When I was in seventh grade, my sisters were a junior and a senior in high school.

Susan, the oldest, seemed to always be in some sort of trouble. You see, my sisters and I are totally opposite, and I'll explain why. Susan was extremely artistic. Her biggest successes while she was growing up were her art-competition wins. Painting, drawing, calligraphy—she could just about do anything artistic. It was a real gift that she had. Not only that but she was also the most intelligent of the three of us too. Susan wasn't really interested in sports; she mainly thought about art, boys, and other things.

Connie, my middle sister, was the most levelheaded. She always was working different jobs. She couldn't wait to leave home and be on her own. My dad and his illness at this time affected my sisters much more than me. When Connie was seventeen, she was going to school and working a full day after that. She would waitress till late at night. During those couple of years, she would drop me off at the junior high school on her way to the high school every morning. I remember her putting on makeup in her room and smoking cigarettes while she did it. Our parents were older. When I was born, my mom was in her late thirties and my dad was around forty. They were fifties kids and saw things differently, so it was no big deal for my sister to smoke in the house or smoke in general, which is amazing to me now because I raise Amelia completely differently. The bottom line is that my sisters were dying to get out of the house, and I was just worried about playing sports and being the next Chris Spielman. (For those of you who don't know, he was an all-American linebacker at Ohio State, and when I was in eighth grade, he was on the cover of the Wheaties box as a senior in high school.)

So when football began in Valwick, it was different from what happened at Oldgrass. In Oldgrass, I played all the time and on both sides of the ball at various positions. I was the same size as and faster than everyone else on the team. Valwick was a bigger town and had more kids; however, now I was much smaller than everyone else and not as fast as them, and those facts were compounded by my being the new kid; none of the coaches knew me. I worked extremely hard to get any kind of playing time. I played some but not a lot. During these three years, I played the most in the "fifth quarter." They would play a whole game, and the kids that didn't get to play very much or at all would play the additional quarter. I never looked down on these opportunities to play—whether it was one play or twenty; I treated all of them as learning opportunities, and I soaked in every piece of experience that I got. I have never forgotten them. After having coached high school football for over twenty years now, I always think of working to get younger kids opportunities to get on the field even a little bit when we have a lead for that experience. Kids that value the game and the opportunity don't and won't forget it and will build upon it. One thing I will say during these three years of playing mostly in fifth quarters, all my coaches always said the same thing. My mom will testify to this because she still speaks of it. A coach would be walking by me as I made my way to the car, and the coach would look at my mom and say, "Your boy loves to hit. He may not be very big right now, but when he is, he will be something."

So these three years pretty much went that way. I rode to school with my sister, went to class, and loved gym and football even though I didn't play as much as I liked. During this time, we lived in an area outside of Valwick; it was a community built around all these little lakes. As someone who grew up on the lake, I would consider them to be more of a series of ponds. I had friends around that I met on the bus, and we would play basketball in one another's driveways or touch football in one another's yards. They had a swimming area in the summer with a platform that you could swim to and dive off of. It was near where I lost my only fistfight. Our bus had junior-high and high-school kids on it for whatever reason. There was a sophomore boy that was nearly six feet tall, and he would pick on junior high kids every day. I was in seventh grade at the time and would spend my ride by looking out the window and minding my own business. Apparently, that day, it was my turn to get picked on. He kept antagonizing me and wouldn't stop. I'm not quite sure where this came from, but I asked him if he wanted to fight, and then I said, "Meet me at the stop sign near the swimming area." He, of course, agreed as any bully would. I marched right down there and proceeded to get my ass kicked. I might as well have been a rag doll. I went home crying, of course, as any twelve-year-old would. On the bus the next day, this boy started bragging about his victory, and I simply laughed and said, "Yeah, you're real tough, beating up a seventh grader." He never picked on anyone again, and I never lost another fight—not that I ever looked for any. These are things that they call "defining moments," and I have had many. Moments when you can make this decision or that and for everyone it is easier to back down however in the long run not backing down or learning to never back down or be persuaded reaps the best rewards.

During those years, when a kid turned fourteen, they could get a moped license. Next thing I knew, the friends that I used to ride bikes with had mopeds. You would hear this little moped gang humming around the lakes. When they would go past our house, I would always look at my dad with a sad face. It seemed like years, but I'm sure that only a few months passed, and one night, while rain was pouring down, I heard this high-pitched honking coming up our gravel driveway. There was my dad; he was riding a used moped in the middle of a thunderstorm with a helmet that was about to fall off his head. I couldn't believe it; I was totally surprised. My dad had one of his friends take him to a neighboring town that was twelve miles away. He bought this moped and then rode it in the pouring rain for twelve miles down two-lane country roads where the speed limit was fifty-five and he could only go thirty miles per hour. As mad as my dad would make me through the years, those are the things I choose to think about because in the end, all of us parents do the very best we can with the skills that we have. Some do better than others, sure, but my dad earned Dad of the Year because of that night. It was funny because the next day, I joined my moped gang, and we tooled around the lakes, and we drove all day and into the night. I remember taking a left turn that night and ending up in the gravel. My first day with my most cherished possession and I crashed it *and* tore my leg up. My dad later asked me what happened to my leg, and I swore up and down that I tackled someone into some stones. He knew I crashed my moped and looked at me as if to say, "You can't bullshit a bullshitter."

CHAPTER 4

GRADE 10—EDGEFIELD

Halfway through my ninth-grade year at Valwick, my dad lost another job, and it was time for us to move again. This time, we went to a large suburb that was even further from the lake. I had only lived in small towns up to this point, so this was completely different. It was an extremely large school district in the city of Edgefield. It was a large division 1 school and was about as big as they get. When I arrived, I had gone from going to Valwick High School to a freshman-only school because it was such a large district. Edgefield had a freshman-only building that led to a campus-style high school that was reminiscent of a college.

In late January 1986, I was in my math class, and they wheeled a television cart into our classroom. We watched the space-shuttle launch. It was especially interesting to the teachers in the school as there was a former schoolteacher among the crew. As many Americans remember, not long into the launch, the shuttle exploded. These are the types of events that make us never forget where we were and when.

Edgefield was extremely intimidating to a kid who had only known small towns. A high school that had over a thousand boys to choose from to play football is much different than a town that only has a few hundred boys to choose from. I attended the football meeting anyway and looked around at all these kids. There were at least fifty freshmen at the meeting.

That spring, in science class, my teacher asked us if anyone was interested in caddying at a local country club. I had never done that; however, I considered it because I would be graduating from riding my moped to driving a car soon, and at that age, it can't happen fast enough. I was well aware that if I wanted a car, I would need to pay for it myself. My science teacher was the "caddy master" at his summer job, so I went and learned how to caddy. I would carry a bag for eighteen holes and make around $20 per round. I soon graduated to carrying two bags for eighteen holes—sometimes even thirty-six holes. I was a very hard worker and responsible, so next thing I knew, they were asking me to work in the pro shop as well. This lifestyle was completely foreign to me, but I grew to like working all the time and making money. Nearly every day that summer, I would carry two bags for eighteen holes from 8:00 a.m. till noon, make my cash for the day, and then work in the pro shop from noon till 8:00 pm. I earned the minimum wage while working in the pro shop; in 1986, that was $3.35 per hour. So I was making over $20 per day with caddying and over $20 per day in the pro shop as well. It didn't bother me a bit that I was working twelve hours a day at fifteen. My mom had a 1980 Dodge Omni, and I wanted to buy it from her. We agreed on the price of $900. I would start giving my mom $20 a day, and I had a handwritten spreadsheet that I would use to record how I would chip away at the total amount owed for the car. This was my first experience of making payments and seeing how it is done. This was also the year when my dad's illness really picked up. My mom would say later, "John got the brunt of it." I saw my dad at his very worst. You see, at this time, both of my sisters were long gone. Susan was going to an art school. Connie graduated high school after the first semester of her senior year and moved out to live on her own at seventeen years old. That's how badly she wanted to get out of the house. So I was the only one left at home with my mom and soon-to-be-extremely-manic dad.

An early example would be the 1980 Dodge Omni that I worked so hard to save money for. And if you do the math, you would know that I would need to pay my mom $20 a day for forty-five days to pay off that car. That is forty-five rounds of golf; I carried two bags. That is 180 hours of work, and I wasn't even sixteen yet. One day, my mom was driving down a busy road; I was in the passenger seat. A man pulled out in front of us, and we broadsided him. All those hours of work wasted on a totaled car. In a normal family, the parent would use the insurance money to buy a different car for their child. They would say, "Son, this is the amount they gave us for the car. Let's go find you a new car." This is not how it works with a seasonal bipolar father. My $900 was gone. My dad pocketed the insurance money and then sold the wrecked car and kept that money as well. At fifteen and getting ready to earn my driver's license, you can imagine my disappointment. This is one of the events that taught me to bounce back and keep climbing. Sometimes you win, sometimes you lose, but you need to keep working every day. Life is very hard even when you try to do everything right.

So this leads up to my sophomore year in high school. I needed to make a decision. I had a very good job. I could either work until snow was on the ground and recoup the money I had lost or play football at a school that had six-foot-four, 280-pound linemen while I was still five feet four and maybe 140 pounds with no chance to play. I already had such limited success at a much smaller school.

I really had a dilemma because I still had it in the back of my mind that I would somehow play in the NFL. I'll be honest—I was intimidated by what I was facing at the school, and working looked like a more viable option to me at that point as I was paying for everything, including my clothes, because I could now work. I didn't play that year and chose to work. I really didn't have any friends either. I would leave at lunch even though we were not supposed to leave the campus and be by myself. On Friday nights, I would ride my moped to the football stadium and stay in the parking lot in order to listen to the announcer on the PA as a game was played. There were two really big games that year, and I listened to them as I sat on my moped. In hindsight, that was the worst fall I ever had because I was physically away from the game I loved.

When spring arrived in 1986, I paid for my driver's education classes myself and soon earned my driver's license. This stands out to me, as it does to every teenager. My dad's mania was getting worse every year because he refused to be medicated. People with this condition think they're invincible during the manic state and that absolutely nothing is wrong. To give you an example of what a manic mind is like, during this particular year, my dad was fired from his job on a Monday. He proceeded to buy two new station wagons by Friday. This isn't what I would call a fiscally responsible decision when we really didn't have extra money in the first place. I know that I paid for every single thing that I wanted outside of food. Shortly after, my mom asked me how I would feel about moving back to Springfall. I thought it would be a great idea because I had friends there, it was a small school, and I knew I would have an opportunity to play football again. I wasn't going to sit out another season ever again. Looking back now, it's funny because I just got my driver's license a month before, and there I was, driving a giant moving truck from Edgefield to Springfall—a trip that takes more than three hours. My mom drove one station wagon, and my dad drove the other. My daughter wasn't allowed to leave the city limits for over a year after she got her license, but I was somehow the king of the road in that huge moving truck.

CHAPTER 5

GRADE 11—SPRINGFALL

When we moved back to Springfall, we rented a huge farmhouse. I was very excited to be back on the lake and to have friends again. While looking back at my sophomore year, I realized I spent most of it not on doing any activities but on working, and I really had no close friends. I was attending football games by staying on my moped in the parking lot by myself for God's sake. So being with my old friends and having more than enough to do was very exciting. That summer was a whirlwind of activity. Whatever I missed out on previously, I made up for in Springfall. I immediately got a job at a restaurant in the community where I had lived in fourth grade. I scrubbed pots and pans for $78 per week. It was not a lot of money, but I was really good at saving, and I needed to be good at that if I wanted another car. I failed to mention earlier that I had gotten my first set of weights in fourth grade and had been using them since. By this time, I had a pretty elaborate weight set in my room. This farmhouse was huge, so there was plenty of room for my bed, dresser, two weight benches, and various dumbbells, and of course I had a mirror so I could gauge my progress.

I soon met up with old friends and got into a daily routine. I wouldn't exactly recommend this routine to my players today, but this was the '80s, and things were different. I would get up and run to the restaurant, which was about three miles from our farmhouse. I would then scrub pots and pans that were used for breakfast. Then they fed me lunch; I had veal parmigiana every single day. To this day, I absolutely love it and order it every chance I get. The restaurant would then serve lunch, and I'd hand-wash all the lunch pots and pans as well. During this time, my hands became capable of handling all kinds of hot-water temperatures. When I finished, I would run home, where my friend Dave would be waiting in my driveway. We would lift weights for an hour. Then we would go to a drive-through, buy a twelve-pack of beer, and find a party. Dave looked much older than I did and would always light a cigarette to appear older, and it worked like a charm at that place. That was my routine every single day of that summer. Looking back on it now, I would die a thousand deaths if my daughter had one beer or was around one cigarette or vape. Any single little thing and she would have absolutely no privileges for a year, and she knows it. I am smart enough to know that the habits you develop when you're young are the ones you keep, so I've worked to teach Amelia to not develop any bad habits while she's still young. I did have friends at that time who would smoke cigarettes and do other bad things; however, I never got into any of those, fortunately. I would simply drink my beers and go along with whatever party we were attending. I never gave in to the temptation. I would simply say no or leave and think nothing of it. Most people aren't like that, I guess. You have to remember that this was a vacation hot spot during the summer. There were different girls around every week, so we were very much into meeting all of them and showing them around.

My dad's mania was so bad that summer. I think my mom's plan was we would move there, my dad would collect unemployment, and she and I would work. She had worked in this area before and knew it wouldn't be a problem. Past that, I don't think my parents had a plan. I also remember waking up for work one morning. I was ready to run to work and looked out to our gravel driveway, and one of those station wagons was gone. I asked about it, and he said it was in the shop. I knew it wasn't. We were headed for a rough winter that year.

Two siblings owned the restaurant where I worked that summer. One was my buddy; he had taken me out on his boat and cooked my lunch every day. The other was someone I didn't talk to much. June and half of July had passed, and I was having the best summer of my life. I knew football two-a-days were going to start in August, so I let them know that I would be quitting so I could play. One of them began to chastise and belittle me and Springfall football, saying it was a joke, and I became very offended. We got into a screaming match right there in the kitchen because I wasn't having it. I quit right then—two weeks early. My buddy then pulled me to the side and said, "Hey, if you need a job until the two-a-days start, you can paint my cottage." It was a big two-story cottage. He agreed to pay me $300 to finish three sides of it. I remember thinking that he was getting a huge deal. I was able to get the job mostly finished in those two weeks, and he did pay me $300. Well, that amount plus the money I had saved allowed me to buy my first car—a 1976 Ford Granada that cost me $500. It wasn't much to look at and was nothing compared to my friends' cars, but there is something to be said for working your ass off for something you want. When it's finally mine, it might as well have been a brand-new Camaro in my eyes.

Football finally started, and I was really excited. I had finally hit puberty and had grown some. I was nowhere near college or pro standards, but for Springfall,

I was a decent size—five feet ten and 160 pounds. Once again, I was the new kid, which I was used to, and it seemed as though they had their lineups already picked out, and I had some catching up to do as far as fundamentals and key reads and such were concerned. I was able to rotate in as a guard that season, play all the special teams, and was a backup linebacker. Midway through the season, I felt I could have started as a linebacker, but that wasn't my decision. I was just happy to finally be playing and contributing. We grossly underachieved, going 5–5 that season. It seems as though my class of juniors liked to party too much and the seniors liked to tell on us too much; we just never really came together as a team.

The season ended and winter came. If you have ever spent a winter on one of the Great Lakes, you would know it is wicked cold. At this point, both my parents were unemployed, and we still lived in the giant farmhouse. My parents couldn't afford to pay for the fuel oil we needed to heat that big house. I remember our landlord giving us a propane heater that we put in the middle of the living room. I'll never forget those months. I would sleep on the couch in front of the propane heater, and my parents would sleep in the bedroom just off that room. There were four panels that you could light up to warm the house. We only lit two of those panels to conserve the propane. I lay there night after night, saying to myself, "I'm never going to live like this." This, for me, was another defining moment. At this time, I couldn't wait for morning to come. I would get up to take a shower, and let me tell you, taking a shower when you can see your breath at the same time isn't very fun. I couldn't wait to get in my '76 Ford Granada and crank the heat up in that thing after shivering all night. I would pick up my friend, and we would head to school. That was my life until my parents really needed to move again.

This time, they wanted to move to Aldbridge, where my dad had found a job at a funeral home in the city. Now I was finally happy, had friends, and was playing football, and I would run track that spring. I didn't want to go at all. I asked my friend Dave if I could stay with his family for the rest of that school year and my senior year. I remember taking him to his house and him going inside to ask his family. I got nervous and drove away. We didn't have a phone in the farmhouse where we lived, so he couldn't call me that night. He spoke to me the next day at school; he said his parents had agreed. I couldn't believe it and was very excited. My mom sat down with Dave's mom, and they came to an agreement. My mom was going to mail $15 to me every week for my school lunch and other school expenses and mail $15 to Dave's parents every week to cover my food. At that time, $15 a week didn't even come close, and they soon found that out. I drank a gallon of milk a day at this point, and the dinners they had were so amazing, I couldn't stop eating. They had a very nice home. Dave's dad was an extremely hard worker. Dave's mom was a secretary at the school. To me, they were extremely wealthy. The fact that I could sit down and eat at their dinner table used to make me so happy. At Christmas, they had gifts for everyone.

Everyone was so warm and loving. It was my first experience of a stable, calm, and hardworking environment. I would be asleep on the living-room floor after falling asleep while watching a movie the night before. I remember the coffee maker starting to brew at 3:30 a.m. and Dave's dad getting his coffee and leaving for work. Most days, he would come home around sixteen hours later, and then he would do it all over again the next day. I paid attention to that and learned what working to provide for your family is really like through that experience.

Spring came and I ran track. I enjoyed track a lot but in a different way than football. I threw the shot put and discus and then ran the hundred meters and two hundred meters. It was an odd combination, but it eventually suited me. My friends and I were still up to our shenanigans. I didn't pay enough attention to my schoolwork because I didn't want to miss any of the fun. Well, this cost me and several of my football teammates. Several of us were deemed ineligible for our senior season of football. I was crushed. I know it was my fault, but I was still devastated. At this point, I didn't know what to do. Summer started, and we all started our summer jobs. For a short time, I didn't want to have any rules, so I moved out of Dave's house and stayed in my own camper with a friend—not a trailer, like the ones found in a trailer park, but a camper. This lasted about a month, and I was fed up with myself. I knew I couldn't keep this up and accomplish any goal I had. It was time for me to get out of there. Don't get me wrong—it was a heck of a lot of fun, but you can't do that every day and think you're going to get somewhere. One day, I didn't even say a word to any of my friends. I just packed up my car and left for Aldbridge.

CHAPTER 6

GRADE 12—ALDBRIDGE

I arrived in Aldbridge in late June 1988. My parents now lived in a very small two-bedroom, one-bathroom apartment. My dad was now employed at a funeral home downtown, and my mom started work at the college in town as a secretary. Instead of getting a job right away, I joined a gym two miles down the road. I began running there every morning and lifting for an hour and running home. I had no friends yet, which was fine because having too much fun was what got me into my previous predicament. I was focused on becoming as big and as strong as I could possibly be. I had it in my head that maybe my new school wouldn't get my grades from Springfall or could maybe let me slide through. We lived in Greenwolf, which was just north of the college campus. My dad, of course, wanted me to visit the Catholic high school there. I called and met with the coach. I looked at the price for tuition and thought there was no way I could go there. I knew my dad would tell me to go there but wouldn't or couldn't pay the bill and didn't want to deal with the embarrassment. I love my dad, and I know he did the best he could, but his illness caused us all a tremendous amount of embarrassment throughout the years. My next call was to the head coach of Cordale. I know now that the coach had played for the great Woody Hayes several years before. I had been working out for weeks and felt very ready. I had grown as well; I was now close to six feet and was 185 pounds. I was still not huge, but compared to my previous five-foot-two freshman body, I'd take it. My 1976 Ford Granada had died, and my sister had given me her old car. Coach said they would be doing drills that evening and told me to come and talk to him. I parked next to the field. I sat there and looked at the players and coaches. Nearly every single person was African American. I was immediately terrified. Keep in mind that I had been going to schools that were 99 percent Caucasian for the last twelve years. I drove off, listening to a Metallica tape that was in my sister's cassette deck. I drove for a while and became angry with myself. I remember hitting the steering wheel and screaming like some kind of insane person. I went home and then went to the gym and worked out. I called the coach again that evening and apologized and said I'd be there the next day. I showed up and was more intense and enthusiastic than I had ever been in my entire life. I was actually more scared than anything else, but in the end, who cares what motivates you? The coaches soon loved me, and so did my teammates. I had African American friends for the first time in my life. It was culture shock, yes, and I couldn't understand the slang, but over time, I was just another kid on the team. No matter where you are, people always appreciate people who know how to work hard. So we attended the camp, and I started on both sides of the ball. I was playing guard and defensive end at the time, and Coach also said I would play fullback if that was needed. It was awesome, and I loved it. We had our first scrimmage, and I had three sacks and a late hit on the quarterback. Everything was going great. I gained a little experience from the previous season, and I was stronger and twenty-five pounds heavier. On the Monday before the second scrimmage, Coach told me to meet him in his office. He said they had received my transcripts from Springfall and they didn't look good but he was going to make some calls. He called and tried to get a couple of teachers to change my grades enough to make me eligible. One did, but the other refused. All of this was embarrassing. The year before, at Springfall, I played in nine games and was ineligible for the tenth. In my mind, at Cordale, I would be ineligible for nine games and be eligible for the tenth. I was going to practice my ass off all season and use that one last game to show someone what I could do. So that's what I did. I practiced every day while going to this inner-city school.

Keep in mind that Cordale was considered as the worst of the worst in this area for public schools. We used to be able to walk down the street to get fast food for lunch, and I witnessed a student get a gun put to his head over a fish sandwich. The perpetrator was on the news that night. I remember pointing him out to my parents. Not a normal conversation when asked "how was school today" "well we went to lunch and . . ." My brother-in-law told me later that the gang members of the school where he was teaching didn't even go near my school; it's that bad. I made a lot of friends, thank goodness, and didn't have too many problems, relatively speaking. Granted, the classes were not ideal. For example, I remember being in history class, and I literally heard kids say *motherfucker* out loud fifteen times. I recall the teacher walking over to me and saying "What do I do with these kids?" I sat there and shrugged, not knowing what to say. All I did all day at Cordale was keep my mouth shut and try to learn. I remember feeling sorry for the teacher. There were good teachers and coaches in this school; however, it is very difficult to educate when you have to discipline so much. I was determined to get my GPA up because it was not good when I arrived at Cordale.

We got to week 10, and I received my report card; it only had As and Bs on it. I was incredibly excited to show what I could do. I had my uniform on and was ready to go. I was called into the coach's office before the game. That year, the state had changed the rule: If you were ineligible at the start of the season, you were ineligible the whole way through. I went to the locker room and was inconsolable. One of my teammates saw me later when we were adults at a coaching clinic, and he shook my hand and told me he never forgot that. I went out for the game, and I remember the coach grabbing my hand with his huge hand and pulling me out so I could go for the coin toss; he made me a captain for that game. It's hard to write about this now. At forty-eight years old, I have tears streaming down my face as I type this.

For a kid who wanted to be just like Chris Spielman, my high school football career wasn't much to write home about. My circumstances and my being a late bloomer were part of the cause, but I also did not take care of business in the classroom, and that was on me.

The school year continued, and Coach had me wrestle that year. It was the first time I had ever wrestled in my life. I wrestled in the 189-pound weight class that year. I was the heaviest on the team, so he—all 265 pounds of him—would wrestle me every day with one hand. He wrestled me with one hand as he had an accident during the football two-a-days that year. He was working in his woodshop and had amputated four fingers of his right hand. He missed one day of practice and returned with them all stitched and pinned back on. He was an incredibly big, strong, tough, hard man. It was no wonder that Woody Hayes had recruited him. Wrestling was very tough, but it was a good experience. I wrestled a three-time state champion and thought I was going to be killed in front of all those people. I wasn't, and it was a miracle that I made it out of the first period at all; he pinned me in the second. I have a picture of me coming out of the locker room after I had the blood wiped off my mouth.

I did track at Cordale as well. I threw the shot put and the discus but didn't run the hundred meters and two hundred meters like at Springfall. These kids were a little—no, a lot faster than Springfall kids. It was a great experience because I got to witness great talent that year. We ran at an invitational that had teams from three states. I remember seeing Chris Nelms run that day; he was a very special talent and went on to run at Ohio State. I always paid attention when I was around real talent.

My senior year came to an end. I finished this year with a 3.5 GPA, bringing my cumulative average up to a whopping 2.1. I applied to two colleges—one big state school and one small community college. During this time, state schools accepted you if you had a heartbeat. Coach had encouraged me to walk-on at the state school, saying they put their pants on one leg at a time like I do. My response was "Yeah, Coach—it's just their pants are a lot bigger than mine." I didn't even know if I was any good; I had not really played against any kind of talent. I was accepted there for the winter quarter, so the small community college it was.

CHAPTER 7

I had played three sports and had gotten outstanding grades at Cordale. I graduated and started working multiple jobs and working out like a crazy person at the gym. I didn't exactly know where I was heading, but I knew I wanted to train and get as big and as strong as possible just in case an opportunity presented itself. That summer, I worked as a lifeguard during the day and as a bouncer at night. The bars hired through the gym many times. My body was really changing from a boy's to a man's, and I hired different trainers who really taught me what I needed to do. This is how the summer after my senior year went with the occasional trip to the lake to visit my old friends. I knew not to make a habit of that, or I would make a habit of that.

The summer ended, and I enrolled at the small college. At first, I was very fortunate in that I won all kinds of scholarships through my school. I went there to pay my first semester's tuition, and they handed me hundreds of dollars back, which was a shock. The biggest problem, I soon realized, with having gone to four different high schools is I had what are known as gaps in education. Going from school A to school B and taking algebra you are not starting at the same spot where you left off and can cause a person to become lost and then move to a lower math for example. I finished all of high school with only Algebra 1. My daughter finished Algebra 2 in eighth grade. These gaps made me struggle in college, especially in math. My other problem was I was not involved in any extracurricular activity of the school. I always liked having coaches because they helped me keep myself on track. I went to school that semester and continued to bounce at the bars. At that time, there was an entire strip of them that lined State Street. I worked at several throughout that whole year. I enjoyed it a lot, and it made me feel somewhat important.

The best thing that happened to me at that college is they placed me with the best adviser I have ever had. His name was Rick Spielman. Remember my childhood hero, Chris Spielman? This was his older brother. I am not very religious, and I am a very bad Catholic. I have prayed hard to God for strength twice in my life. After living for forty-eight years, I can say now that someone puts people in your life at different times, and this is part of a plan for you. Rick Spielman was put in my life at this time for a reason. He would talk to me daily about just showing up at a college to play if that's what I wanted to do. He would give me examples of kids that he had advised that had done that. We would talk about lifting, supplements, etc. He would talk about how he and Chris would bet a sleeve of Copenhagen as to who would have more tackles in their game against a common opponent; they went to different schools. One day, I was leaving his office, and I almost ran headfirst into Chris, my hero. My mouth fell open. He was maybe an inch taller than I was. His chest was as big as a barrel, but he wasn't much taller than me. I thought I could make my chest big and thought I wouldn't need to grow much taller. I am convinced that these men were placed in front of me at the time I needed them the most to help guide me to where I needed to go. I am forever grateful for them passing through my life.

I completed one semester of college and did not do well, so I decided to drop out. I was now competing in powerlifting competitions and winning, becoming extremely strong in the process. I was still bouncing at the bars at night and started being a hod carrier during the day. A hod carrier is basically a bricklayer's assistant. A man asked me if I was interested in working as one and if I wanted to give it a shot one day, and I agreed. He said, "Shovel this gravel off this flatbed. I'll be back." I shoveled this entire flatbed full of gravel in a very short period of time, and he was amazed. He offered me a job that would pay $7 an hour. I jumped on it because in 1990, that was great money. From January to July, that's all I did. I laid bricks from 8:00 a.m. to 4:00 p.m., trained at the gym at 5:00 p.m., and bounced at the bar from 8:00 p.m. to 2:00 a.m. I was hired periodically to work different concert venues, which was also fun. For whatever reason, they would put me dead center at the front the majority of the time. It was funny because I never had enough money to spare to pay for a concert, and the only ones I attended were the ones I worked on. I worked some big concert venues. I would get a weekend off here and there during the summer. Whenever I did, I would drive to that lake and that peninsula. I loved seeing my old friends. At this point, no one could believe I was the same person; I had become so muscular. Everyone thought I was on steroids, but I wasn't. One weekend, I was visiting my friend Dave, and we were getting ready to head out for the day. His uncle was there, and he was a successful basketball coach from a big city in the state. First, he asked me if I still wanted to play football. I said, "Absolutely, but no one wants me."

He told me of a coach named Randy Stoltz, who was starting a division 3 football program in Shadowmont. He stated that he had been the head coach at Miami of Ohio, he had taken Indiana to the Rose Bowl, and he had been the head coach at Northwestern and Yale. I asked, "What he's doing at a division 3 school?"

He said, "He's sixty-four years old and wants the challenge."

I told Nolan I'd think about it and went on to the islands to have a good time.

I drove home; I felt refreshed and ready to get back to work and working out. I laid bricks that Monday and then went home and showered. I ran to the gym and lifted. I ran back home that evening. I put a dip in and thought, *I'm going to call this coach*. Nolan had given me Coach Stoltz's number. I called him, and we set an appointment for 11:00 a.m. that Friday.

CHAPTER 8

MEETING COACH STOLTZ

I had never been to Shadowmont in my life. I, of course, had heard of schools in Shadowmont that won many state football titles, and I, of course, heard of the pro teams in that area, but that was about it. I drove down in a 1976 Pontiac Sunbird with no front-left quarter panel. It was like a tire out in space. I bought that car that summer for $1,168. If you're wondering how I remember the prices of these cars, it's because I always valued every penny and had to work my ass off to buy these vehicles by myself.

I arrived on the campus of Big Valley Academy over two hours early. I walked the campus, making sure I would know where to go to meet Coach Stoltz and be on time. I went to what I would later come to find out was the classroom building. There were these glass double doors there. The craziest thing happened. I opened those doors to walk down that hallway, and I smelled a smell that I hadn't had for a long time. It was the smell of my first Catholic grade school. It was overwhelming to me at the time. I went to school at this academy for four and a half years and never smelled that smell again. If there are such things as signs, that was definitely a sign to me, especially since I went there after and never smelled it again.

I walked the whole campus and was still incredibly early, so I decided to drive and find a place to stop in. I wasn't hungry, but I sat there and drank a milkshake, wondering if this would be where I would end up. I definitely needed something, and I didn't want to lay bricks my whole life; I knew that. I killed some time there with that milkshake and then drove back to the campus. I checked in with the secretary, and she let Coach Stoltz know I was there. Coach Stoltz was a small man with an enormously large presence and a deep voice. I heard him say, "John, come on in." He greeted me, shook my hand, and had me take a seat. I took one look at his Big Ten championship ring and the picture of him shaking hands with the president and knew I was going there. While he was talking, in my head, I was saying, *I don't know how much this place costs or how hard I have to work. Those don't matter. I'm coming here and playing my ass off for this man.* I knew right there and then. Coach Stoltz would be the second coach I had played for who was coached by Woody Hayes. Coach Hayes coached Randy Stoltz at Miami of Ohio prior to being hired by Ohio State. Both coaches are now in the Cradle of Coaches. There are several all-time coaches that have come from that university.

I had lunch with Coach Stoltz, and we talked for an hour or so before going back to his office. He then asked me what position I wanted to play. I had a little experience of playing a lot of positions. He comforted me by saying, "Our job is to put you in the best position possible to be successful." I had no doubt that he would do that.

This meeting happened just after the Fourth of July weekend. That was my reason for going to the lake. We reported to camp on August 1. So I applied to the college in a hurry, and I needed to train even harder to get ready. I applied and was accepted. I found out later that every single young man who put *football* on their application was accepted. I was really excited! During those last three weeks of summer, I added a new wrinkle to my training. I would go and train at the gym just like always but would then go to Ohio Stadium every day. At that time, they had ten-foot-high iron fences with a pointed top on all the bars. I would climb this fence every day to get into the stadium and run the steps of the Shoe. In hindsight, I was fortunate to not have been impaled while climbing that huge thing. I would run up and down adjacent to every walkway on the bleachers for the entire U of the Horseshoe. I had been working out so hard for so long, I was now six feet tall, 215 pounds, and all muscle. I had finally matured physically. I remember that one day, as I was running the stadium, I saw Steve Tovar (an Ohio State linebacker who later played in the NFL), who was there with a girlfriend. He asked me if I played football. I told him I was getting ready to go to Big Valley Academy in Shadowmont. He said he thought I was going someplace bigger. That told me that I at least looked the part.

The day came; it was time for me to move into the dorms and report to camp. I had gone on a shopping spree with the money I had made from laying bricks. I bought my own fridge and stereo. My dad followed me with a station wagon loaded with my stuff. When we arrived, we unloaded all my stuff onto a big cart. I looked at my dad and said, "See ya!" I couldn't wait to take control of my own life. I didn't have to worry about moving in the middle of the year because I controlled my destiny now. When I was saying "See ya!" one of my later roommates, Joe, was chasing his parents' car while crying. Coach Hubinski grabbed him and said, "Let 'em go, baby. Let 'em go." Joe was clearly more coddled than me, or as my dad would say, he grew up "sucking hind tit."

After moving in, going to the cafeteria to eat, and our first team meeting that night, I went to look around at everyone in camp. More than half were from Shadowmont and the huge schools there. I saw dozens of East–West All-Star shirts; these guys were the best on their high school teams. I was just hoping at this point that I could work harder than everyone else and get a spot on one of the special teams.

We did a lot of testing prior to that first camp. We had strength and speed tests, and I soon found out that all the training I had done had paid off. I was just as strong as the strongest guys there and faster than anyone my size. Things were looking good as we were going into practices. I remember Coach Randol pulling me to the side and asking me if I ever thought about playing linebacker. I said I had played that position a bit and all my heroes had played linebacker, such as Chris Spielman and also Jack Lambert; I was a huge Steelers fan as well.

The great thing about college that was much different than the small high schools I had gone to is every position had an individual coach. We had individual practice times and individual meeting times. Everything we had to do was explained in detail. I was like a sponge—soaking information up as fast as the coaches would give it to me. I was playing harder and faster than I ever had. In college, you have to because every guy there was the best guy on their high school team. I obviously had to do everything better than everyone else because I was next to nothing or felt like next to nothing on all four of my high school teams.

1,2,6 as i like to say i was starting at inside linebacker. I was calling home telling my mom "holy shit," I'm going to start game 1 vs. Rose holman college mom!" I felt amazing and was getting better and better.

CHAPTER 9

THE BOMB GOES OFF /
FRESHMAN YEAR

I suppose you understand how seriously I was taking this opportunity. During camp, when my teammates would go out, I would stay in my dorm, go to bed super early, and be up at 3:30 a.m. I couldn't wait to hit people every single day. On the inside, I was the same junior-high kid who loved to hit. On the outside, I was a pretty big, strong, fast man, so the two things matched pretty well. The next day, at practice, Coach Stoltz had an announcement for us. I had no clue what he was talking about. I didn't really socialize with anyone, so I didn't hear any gossip. He said, "Don't any of you worry. We will be fielding a team this year. I will be calling some of you to my office to talk this evening."

I had no clue what the heck he was talking about.

Remember when I told you that if you put *football* on your application, you got in? That was literally true. We had guys who got 3s on their ACTs, guys who struggled badly to read and write, guys who had been in the navy, guys who had been married and divorced, and guys like me who spent a semester at Aldbridge State Community College and whose grades did not transfer in and the ones that did were Ds, which deemed me and a dozen others academically ineligible. It was happening again, but this time, I completely didn't expect it. I was overwhelmingly devastated! This is the first of two times in my life that I found myself praying hard to God; I prayed as if my life depended on it. I went to the church on campus, and I was in their front row and on my knees, crying and whispering with folded hands, "Please, God, give me the strength to get through this!" I said it over and over. It would have been very easy for me to just quit and go to a cheaper school, but that thought never entered my mind. I pulled myself up by my bootstraps and went back to work. It was difficult to go from being a starter to a scout-team player, but I did it. I made up my mind; I told myself that this would become a time for me to get better. I treated practices like actual games and went all out, giving the offense fits that made them better in the end. I did that all fall, and after we got off the bus from our last game that season, Coach Heizma pulled me to the side and said, "You get your grades right, and next season, you'll have ten tackles every game."

Remember, I had a lot of gaps in my education, so I had to really study, prepare, and pay attention. When kids ask me for advice before they enter college, I always say, "Go to every single class. I don't care if it's an 8:00 a.m. class and you were out till 4:00 a.m. the night before. You go to every class." So that's what I did. My grades weren't great at first, but I was able to earn better and better grades every semester I went to college. I was finally settled and comfortable and cared about. They made me feel like I had a real home and I controlled the end of this story.

So that year, I continued to train like crazy and attend every class. After the first semester, I was called to the guidance office. They said I needed to declare a major. Frankly, this never occurred to me. I told them to just sign me up for anything that would keep me eligible. I only went to that school to play football and never even thought about the career I would have after that. In their wisdom, they asked me for what I liked to do. I said I liked to work out and play football. They suggested physical education. I said "Fine," not thinking anything about it. Next thing I knew is I was in a gym with a man in his late sixties who talked to me and my classmates as if we were eight-year-olds. Mind you, at this point, I felt like I was the baddest man on the planet and no one would speak to me this way. He continued as I was getting more and more mad, and then it dawned on me: *Holy shit, I'm going to be a gym teacher? I guess that will be OK.*

Right now, my daughter is finishing her senior year in high school. She has been doing an internship for the past two years as a special educator. She has a very clear and defined career path and will be able to coach gymnastics, cross-country, swimming, diving, and track and field with a specialty in pole vault. She has grown up while knowing that school is the most important thing since she was two years old. That's the difference. My parents were trying to survive day to day, week to week, month to month, and year to year, so school was never really on top of the list at all, and I got that. I've been trying to make sure Amelia wasn't like that, and I think I have done OK.

I am very thankful for my college advisers, especially Mrs. Sabinski, who held my hand whenever I registered for a class. I would go in there with a schedule that had the classes that all my friends were taking. She would look at me, smile, tear up that schedule, and say, "Now this will be what you're really taking." And then she would write it all out for me. She would then ask how the football was going. She was the greatest, and I would later coach football against her son and always ask about her and reiterated that she got me through school.

They really did give me great advice. If anyone has a kid who doesn't know what they want to do after college, simply ask them, "What do you love to do?" When they give you an answer, research employable occupations that have them doing that. Then they will never really work a day in their life.

I finished that first year of college with a 2.76 grade-point average. It was not great, but I was finally going to be eligible to play! I went home to my parents' apartment in Aldbridge. I picked up where I left off; I laid bricks all day, lifted at the gym, ran in the Ohio Stadium, and bounced at the bars at night. I did that all June and July until it was time to report to camp in August.

CHAPTER 10

PLAYING COLLEGE FOOTBALL

I showed up to camp in August 1991 and was ready to go. After all those years, everything was now falling into place. I reassumed the starting role I had lost the year before, and we regained all the other players who were deemed ineligible as well, which made us a better team. Summer two-a-day practice was great, and I loved all of it. I have always loved every part of football. What I mean by that is I loved winter, spring, and summer training. I loved practice, which a lot of players don't care for, and I loved the games, but everyone loves those. There were days during that summer camp that were really difficult, and I will point one out in particular as it will become important later. There was one day that was exceedingly difficult. I had been hitting a lot and working very hard. College football was much, much more physical than anything I had experienced in high school—not to mention that I hadn't really played much in high school. I remember that after breakfast, while I was walking to my locker, it felt like everything hurt. From the bottoms of my eyeballs to the tips of my toes, everything was extremely sore. I remember sitting in my locker and thinking, *There is no way I can make it through this today.* Then I got dressed, put my pads on, laced up my cleats, and went to work. We warmed up, stretched out, and started banging, and I did make it through when I thought I was not going to. This would become a defining moment in my life.

That would prove to be an important day because it became a common theme throughout my college years. Every Saturday that season and every season I ever had, I would play my heart out. I played an exhausting style, not taking plays off and giving everything on every down. Then after the games, win or lose, we would all get together somewhere, drink beer, and look for girls. On Sunday mornings, whenever I woke up, that feeling would come back. I got extremely sore from the bottoms of my eyeballs to the tips of my toes. You grow to love that feeling after a while; if you feel it, you know you have accomplished something.

That freshman season, I had 107 tackles and 2 interceptions in 9 games. Coach Heizma was right when he said I would have 10 tackles a game; well, I had 11.88 tackles a game. Not bad for a kid who never really played before.

That freshman season was very fun and very rewarding. I had a game with twenty tackles too. What was more important was that this year, I was becoming better at being a student. I was still attending every class and discovering classes that I was really interested in. I took to the anatomy, physiology, and kinesiology classes. I was interested in understanding how the human body worked because I liked to work out and wanted to see if I could make myself a better player somehow through this.

That winter, our wide-receiver coach approached me with a job proposition. His brother, Rocky Tekulve, had been an athletic trainer of the Shadowmont Bengals. He had some investors that played for the Bengals, and they were developing a speed-and-agility center that was revolutionary in 1991. They had two treadmills that went up to a forty-degree incline and twenty-six miles per hour. They had workout levels that an athlete could progress through. Each level had twelve workouts and took six weeks. You would speed-train on the treadmill twice a week combined with one day of plyometrics. The job offer involved working there on the evenings and weekends and in the summer, and I'd be able to train for free in my off hours. Keep in mind that parents who would send their kids there were paying $300 per session, and there was no way I could do that with only the money I made through work-study. I thought this was the greatest job ever and took full advantage of the opportunity. I enjoyed training the kids on plyometrics and documenting their workouts. I also loved the training and competing against my own personal best times. In addition to this, I would strength-train with a local PE teacher who was also a master strength coach during the off-season. He got me involved with high-intensity training, which was very different from the powerlifting that I had done before. This combination proved to be valuable in the upcoming years as I became a six-foot, 227-pound athlete who ran a 4.71 forty. At division 3, that was very impressive and not often seen.

I finally knew I could play football and play well. I knew how to train to get better and better. I also knew that every semester, I had to go to the bursar's office and sign loan papers that I would have to pay back six months after graduation. I also knew that my mom worked at the state university and I could go there for free. I had always dreamed of going to Ohio State and playing in the Ohio Stadium. I had met Chris Spielman in person and knew that he wasn't more than an inch taller than I was. I scheduled a meeting with Coach Stoltz to talk to him about what I was thinking. Coach Stoltz had coached at both Indiana and Northwestern, so I valued his opinion. We talked for a while, and I explained my position. He just looked at me and said with his big, bold voice, "John, six-foot, 227-pound linebackers are a dime a dozen at Ohio State. You can be Chris Spielman here." In other words, I would be just another guy at that level and a great player who plays all the time at the division 3 level. So I let that go and focused on my next three seasons to see what happened.

That summer, I received a call from Coach Stoltz. We had a player transfer in from Akron that Coach Stoltz had coached at Hamilton High School. He was a former state Defensive Player of the Year in high school. I'll be honest—he was a physical gift from God. The purpose of his call was to ask me if I would be OK with moving from inside linebacker to outside linebacker to solidify our defense. I always agreed with everything Coach Stoltz said, so I didn't question any of it. However, if they had left me where I was, no one would ever have had more tackles than me in the history of the program; that's the way I feel.) At outside linebacker, you really only have a chance at tackles mostly on that side of the field; at inside linebacker, you can truly run from sideline to sideline. The one thing at outside linebacker that was better is having the ability to rush the passer.

So my sophomore and junior years came and went. I continued to improve in my classes, earning 3.0 and above during these years. I had passed my preteaching exam and started doing my teaching practice in various local schools to learn what my future career was going to be all about. In January, after my junior season, the head coach called me to his office. This was now Coach Brian Randel as Coach Stoltz had accepted a position he could not refuse in Japan. I walked into his office and sat down. He told me a scout was coming to see me. I said, "From where? Canada?"

He said, "No, John, the NFL."

I know my eyes got big and my heart definitely started beating fast. He said, "He wants to come in to give you the Wonderlic test [a cognitive-ability test that the NFL gives to players before the draft], time you in the forty, and get some measurements."

I could not believe my ears. I walked out of his office, grabbed the first phone I saw, and called my mom. I was crying while telling her the news; I think we both were. This was in no way any kind of guarantee of anything, but considering where I had come from and all the talented players on my team and on the teams we played against, the fact that I was the only one getting visited was amazing to me. I needed to get ready for this visit, and it wasn't going to be easy.

During the seventh week of the previous season, we played at Olivet Nazarene University, which is outside of Chicago. I was chasing the quarterback toward our sideline, and a receiver cracked back and put his helmet right outside of my right knee. I was lying on our sideline, screaming in pain. I remember looking at the scoreboard and seeing there were sixteen seconds left in the half. When the pain subsided, they got me up and told me to try to jog down the sideline. The bottom half of my right leg was swaying side to side as I ran as if it were blowing in the breeze. I said to myself, "Holy shit, this is serious." They got me in at halftime, and the trainer said there was a lot of movement in my knee. I proceeded to go on a barrage of profanity, insisting that they put a brace on my knee and get me back on the field. The trainer asked the head coach what he thought he should do. Our head coach, God love him, said, "You better do what he's saying." So I finished that game. Then the next two weeks, I didn't practice—just worked on strengthening my knee—but I played both games. At the awards banquet on the Sunday after that last game, I could barely walk to the podium. The head coach praised my toughness and how I was the epitome of what it is to play through pain.

When my visitor from the NFL was set to arrive, I was still not 100 percent healed, but I wasn't going to let that stop me. He first asked me a series of questions. One was "Have you ever been injured?" I said I had a grade 2 strain of my medial collateral ligament and a torn meniscus in my right knee. He then asked me how many weeks I was out. I responded, "Sixteen seconds." This caused Coach Piper, our defensive-back coach who was sitting in the corner and listening in on everything, to start belly-laughing. The week I had my injury, I remember there was an NFL player who had the same thing and was out for three weeks. He then gave me the Wonderlic test, did my height barefoot toes turned out and up off the ground and weight, and took me to the tennis courts in the pouring rain and forty degrees. I remember that I ran a 4.8 that day even with those conditions and a knee that wasn't 100 percent. Regardless, no matter what had happened, I made it onto the NFL's radar, and that is not an easy task, especially in division 3 college football.

During my senior season, in a match against Bluffton, I recorded five sacks—a record that has not been broken even now—thirty years later. My twenty-tackle game is just behind the school record of twenty-one, which was set by the previously mentioned state Player of the Year who transferred in from Akron.

By the time I was finished, I had recorded 276 tackles, 17 sacks, and 2 interceptions. I was all-district three times and first team twice. I was invited to a college-football all-star game in Louisville, Kentucky, where I got to play with players from Ohio State, Memphis, Kansas State, Iowa, and all kinds of other places. I participated in another combine at this game as well. While I was involved with this experience, I took a good look at everyone around. I remember saying to myself, "This guy is just as good as me, and he's going to Europe to play." I did that on multiple occasions. In the end, I came to the realization that I did the absolute best I could do. I maximized my genetics, and my best wasn't good enough for the NFL. It gave me a sense of closure.

My senior season wasn't easy by any means. It wasn't what it is like for division 1 college players, I mean. I had one semester of student teaching to complete, and I needed to work to pay my bills. So I want any parent out there to think about this when they feel like spoiling their kids. I would teach all day and then practice college football. I would then grab fast food and work as a custodian until 11:00 p.m. That was every weekday during my senior season, and I played on Saturday.

Like I told you, I would be sore from the bottoms of my eyeballs to the tips of my toes and didn't feel OK again until the following Wednesday. So there I was, trying to hurt people on Saturday, and on Monday, I was doing the Hokey Pokey with a bunch of first graders. Nothing about that was easy. In fact, the game where I had five sacks, I skipped school that Friday so I could sleep all day and actually feel good for a game. Hard work works for kids, I believe. Learn it early and live it.

CHAPTER 11

MY FIRST YEAR OF TEACHING

I graduated from Big Valley Academy in December 1994—four and a half years from the time I stepped foot on campus. I often describe it as thus: I went there and played football for five years, and they handed me a degree. If I didn't have all those great advisers, I would have ended up with a degree in liberal arts or something that wouldn't be useful in the real world. I graduated with a bachelor of arts degree. I was licensed and certified to teach physical education and health education at any grade level of K–12. I had passed all the necessary teaching praxis exams, which was a feat in and of itself. Remember my gaps in education. I never really learned any math beyond Algebra 1. I was required to pass a statistics class in college, and I barely got through it with a D. So how I passed the math portion of my teaching exam, I'm not exactly sure other than the fact that I have always had common sense, and from lifting weights, I can calculate numbers fairly quickly in my head. The rest was lucky guessing on that particular day.

So I graduated in December, which made it hard for me to get a teaching job right away. At this time, I lived in a house with four other football players in Price Hill. The area is on the west side of Shadowmont. Three of us were going to be teachers, so we all began substitute-teaching every day after Christmas and through the spring. Every morning, we were waiting for the phone to ring to send us to the various schools in varying school districts. We would iron our shirts on the kitchen table with the occasional mouse running by our feet. We rented this house for $400 per month, which was $80 a man.

When summer came, we stayed in that same house and got jobs of roofing houses. It was hard work, which I liked; however, I was working with some different hombres. These guys' lives involved pounding coffee in the morning before getting to the job, getting to work on the job, and by late morning, smoking marijuana on the job. I swear they did this so they could smoke that stuff twenty to eighty feet off the ground and no one else would smell it. We would finish work, and these guys would pull in a drive-through to buy cases of beer that they would put in the back of the truck and quarts of beer that they drank on the way to the shop. Once we got back, we went our separate ways, but it was well documented that they would drink till two, three, or four in the morning and then start it all over again at 6:00 a.m. Those guys did that six days a week; my friend Collin and I worked five days. That's how we spent that summer—roofing houses and applying to every school district in Shadowmont and the surrounding areas.

One day, my phone rang; a district on the east side of Shadowmont needed a junior-high physical-education and health-education teacher. It was a smaller district with a majority of farm-type kids. All I knew was I needed a job and needed to get busy with a career. They offered me the job, and I took it immediately. Lots of people I knew at the time wanted to teach only at the premier districts and were willing to sub another year or more to get that. I didn't think that way. I wanted to get into the state-teachers retirement plan, have insurance, etc. I figured that my work would speak for itself and I would eventually get to where I wanted to be financially. I got my first job in 1995; my contract was for $19,900, and I was to coach junior high football and junior high track for maybe another $2,400 combined. When my friend and I got our first actual checks for teaching, we looked at each other and said we were making more from roofing houses! We didn't understand that roofing houses paid no insurance, retirement, etc.

When I was offered the job, I had a lot of paperwork to fill out, and I found myself in the high-school weight room and signing things. I then met the high school's football coaching staff. They took me in immediately and made me feel at home. They didn't often get guys to coach junior high who had my playing experience in a rural area like this. Some of those same guys have been my great friends for the past twenty-five years. I have attended the Ohio State-football finals the past twenty-five years, and that tradition started with the friendships I made during this first year of coaching.

My first experience with kids in this district happened when junior high football began. The seventh and eighth grades would practice together in a field about 150 yards behind the junior high building. It was only me and a guy named Todd Smith, who was the son of an administrator in the district. Todd was a very by-the-rules kind of guy, having a mom who was in the hierarchy of the district. One day, one of the players chose to talk back to me. At the end of practice, I pulled him aside and told him I was not to be disrespected like that and not to make that choice again or he would not like the outcome. The next day came, and he was goofing around in the huddle, and I snapped at him. He proceeded to call me a prick. I, of course, didn't take this very well and told him to take off all my equipment, go to the school, get his stuff, and go home. I was done with this kid. Two minutes later, we were practicing, and Todd tapped me on the shoulder and said, "Look." The kid was walking back to the school in nothing but his underwear. My head dropped immediately, and I thought to myself, *Oh my goodness.* Todd then proceeded to tell me that the kid's father just got out of prison for assault. My first week at my brand-new job and I made a kid walk 150 yards in his underwear, and his dad was going to want to assault me. Sure enough, twenty minutes later, Todd tapped me on the shoulder again, and here comes the kid and his dad. So I immediately thought to myself that there was absolutely no way I was getting my ass kicked in front of all these kids, and if the worst-case scenario did happen, I could go back to roofing houses. The boy and his dad walked up to us, and the dad said, "My boy tells me you had him walk off in his skivvies."

I explained what had happened and informed the father that it happened after his son called me a prick. The dad looked at his son and said, "Boy, did you call this man a prick?"

He said, "Yes, because that's what he is—a prick!"

The father turned to me and said, "I'm sorry to have bothered you." He then turned and dragged his son back across that field.

That's the thing that I did like about that district, and I was only there for a year: Right was right and wrong was wrong, and the community really got that.

Soon after, the school year started, and I was making a long commute from the west side and my college house to the east side and this small junior-high school. I would teach and then coach and then go home to all my buddies. I coached junior high football but would scout on Friday nights for the varsity and report back to the head coach at his house that evening. He would have all the coaches over to eat, drink beer, and watch that night's game. Also during this time, my friends and I were enthralled with the O. J. Simpson case. Every night, we would watch it. The whole country was fascinated and wanted to know how this would turn out. So weeknights were watching OJ, and Friday nights were high school football.

When the season ended, I became close friends with the high-school defensive coordinator, Zac. He and I had a running date every Wednesday after school. We would meet at a place called the Lost Pelican every Wednesday all winter. It was great. We would walk in, and the bartender would say, "Pitcher?" We would say, "Yep," and he'd bring it over. Zac and I would sit for hours, talking about playing football, how much we missed it, and transitioning to coaching. We developed a lifelong bond in a very short period of time.

Also that winter, something fortunate happened to me. The assistant principal at the school nominated me for the leadership-development academy at the Academy of Shadowmont. Administrators that had been through this program could nominate teachers that they felt would be good administrators. It was a full-scholarship program that one could complete in one year. I had to be nominated, and then I had to apply and be interviewed to see if I was accepted. I did all of those things, and I was informed that I had earned the scholarship! I went to school that next summer full-time. While I was there, I met a teacher from one of the prominent and growing districts in Shadowmont called Townsend.

This, for me, was a game changer!

CHAPTER 12

MY BIG BREAK IN TEACHING

She asked me why I was teaching where I was and told me I should absolutely apply at Townsend. The suburb was growing like crazy, and they were hiring a lot of people. I did what she suggested and was interviewed, and I was immediately offered a job at one of their four junior high schools for a half-time teaching position. Half-time at Townsend would pay nearly the same as my previous district, and I would be getting my master's full-time in the evenings, so it worked out great. Halfway through the year, they wanted me to teach one class at the high school in addition to the junior high. So my half-time job turned into a 90-percent-time one, plus I coached junior high football and later coached high school track. Things were really progressing at a rapid pace. In 1996, Townsend had one high school, and it was overflowing with kids. They were building two brand-new, state-of-the-art high schools that were set to open in 1997. I definitely wanted to teach at the high school and coach varsity football and varsity track and do whatever else I could do. The one class I was teaching at the old high school in Townsend was just what I needed to get my foot in the door. I also scouted for the varsity and got to know all the coaches. I would go to practice, and they would ask me for my opinion. Townsend was a division 1 football program, which is as big as it gets in Ohio. I had never seen a program like that in a high school, so when they asked me for what I thought of it, I said it's just like a college one, and it was. They had kids that only played one way, and every player had an individual coach.

In the spring of 1997, I was offered a health-teaching full-time job at Townsend North High School, I graduated with a master's degree in educational administration from the Academy of Shadowmont, and I bought my own condo in Townsend. I was accomplishing every goal I had made for myself at a very rapid pace.

I had been driving junk cars my entire life, and it was now time for me to get myself a decent car. Dave's dad worked at Ford, and I knew how much he cherished Thunderbirds, which made me want to get one. I found out what the value of a '95 Thunderbird was, and I remember taking out a signature loan at the Townsend County Credit Union for $12,000. I took that amount and wrote a check to Beechmont Ford prior to ever walking into the place. That was the amount I was going to pay and would not spend a penny more. In their mind, I was paying in cash, and as you should know, cash is king, and no dealership wants to see a sale walk out the door. I had been reading all these financial books that said that you must never buy a brand-new car because you lose so much money as soon as you drive off the lot. They said that if you purchase a car that is three years old, you only have to pay 66 percent of the original price, and you're still driving what is basically a new car.

I lived by this principle then and always will. It's a no-brainer no matter how much money you have. The book *The Millionaire Next Door* was the graduation gift I got from my mom. So I walked into the dealership after I found a '95 Ford Thunderbird in the lot. I met with a salesman, and we went back and forth for close to two hours. I told them I would give them a $12,000 check and my trade-in, which at that time was an '87 Nissan Pulsar that was nothing but problems. The salesman kept going back to his boss and would come back with a counteroffer. I never flinched; I never wavered. I knew what I wanted and how much I was willing to pay, and I was not budging. I threatened to leave a couple of times, and by the end, the salesman was practically begging me to come up with even $200 because he was worried about his commission. I did not change my mind during that entire transaction, and I drove that same car for thirteen years, putting over three hundred thousand miles on it. I drove it until the transmission fell out of it. That's how you get your money's worth out of an automobile.

It was the 1997–1998 school year, and I was two years removed from playing college football and earning my bachelor's degree. Since that time, I have earned a master's degree, bought my first home (a two-bedroom, two-bath condo in an up-and-coming suburb), have a "new" three-year-old car, and am making plans to take more classes. In the teaching and coaching profession, to make any kind of money, you have to understand that the salary schedules work vertically and horizontally. What that means is that for every year you teach, you make more money vertically on the scale. The more education you get or degrees you have, the more you move horizontally on that scale. It was easy for me to deduce that I needed to get as much education as I could as fast as I could. Townsend paid up to master's then master's +15 then masters +30 semester hours. So in my mind, since I had my master's, in the 1997–1998 school year, I'd take 15 more that year and 15 more in 1998–1999 school year and spend my career maxed out. I would also coach everything I could to add those supplemental contracts to this. I had contracts for coaching varsity football and varsity track and eventually had one for head strength and conditioning coach for a school.

What that means is that in addition to being paid as much as possible for teaching because of my education, I also always made another five digits for coaching on top of that. To a lot of people, especially these days, this is a lot or too much work for them. To me, it really wasn't that big of a deal. I really loved what I was doing, so it wasn't work for me at all. Hard work was all those things I had to do in college and high school. I added them up later, and I found out that I had worked close to fifty different jobs prior to becoming a teacher. Lay bricks all day, work out, and then bounce at a bar till two o'clock in the morning—that's hard work. Teaching and coaching was and is fun, so I get confused when I hear teachers complain about how stressed they are. It's laughable especially when all they do is teach and there is no coaching involved. If they are this stressed and it is so hard for them, it seems to me that their advisers in college didn't give them as much great advice as I had gotten and they should be in another profession.

I bought my first computer in 1995 for $1,900. Today, you could get a fantastic computer for that amount of money. This is when the Internet really first started. But I used this computer every single morning to look at my goals. I made a spreadsheet of what I was making that year from teaching, coaching football, coaching track, and strength and conditioning. I forecasted my income for the next five years and made sure to stick with my plan to accomplish my educational goals. I also had Quicken, a program that I used to manage my checking account, savings account, Roth IRA, car payment, student loans, etc. I would track all of them. I did have debt during that time, and I hated it. I would work very hard to overpay on the smallest ones and, as Dave Ramsay would say, snowball toward the biggest debts. I always kept in mind the memory of being sixteen in that farmhouse, lying on the couch and seeing those two lit propane panels while I was freezing. Those thoughts never left me, and they're why I was so obsessed with earning and paying attention to my finances. I was very happy and well on my way to being very successful in the career I had chosen.

CHAPTER 13

MEETING HER

It was the 1998–1999 school year. (Teachers remember everything by school year; at least this one does.) I had dated various people, but none of these relationships became serious. I never had a relationship that lasted more than a year. I was usually too involved in football or trying to make money to pay enough attention to any one person. I was in my fourth year of teaching; in some ways, I felt totally in control, and in others, I felt completely out of control. All my financial things were progressing great; however, in the back of my mind, I really missed playing football. Coaching helped with that, but whenever I had downtime or had nothing to do, I would drink too much—whether I was out with friends or home alone. If I had nothing pressing the next day, I would drink beer until every single one was gone—no matter how many were in the fridge. I generally had control in every relationship I was ever in. Not that I was controlling—just that if anyone remotely tried to tell me what to do, I would have none of it and let them know that or just leave the relationship altogether.

At the time, all my college friends were getting married, and on the inside, I felt like I was out of control. Looking back on it, I think I was just a normal twenty-seven-year-old single man who had accomplished a lot even though he came from so little. My friend Dave, the one I had lived with in Springfall, had graduated and was now living with his future wife in Ohio, just outside of Aldbridge. He called me and wanted me to come up and go out with him. He and I went to a bar, drank, talked, and played pool. His future wife, Susan, had gone out with her friend, Roseanne, that same night. After a couple of hours, he asked me if I wanted to go to his house and play euchre with the girls. The next thing I knew, we were drinking, playing euchre, and talking. I noticed that Roseanne kept giving me shit, which was completely out of the norm for me. I didn't know if I liked it or hated it at the time. She was very argumentative and wouldn't stop until she thought she had won the argument. I didn't care much about it and thought, *If I get laid, great. If not, I'm going home tomorrow anyway.* Not exactly love at first sight. Dave and Susan went to bed, and we were left alone in the living room. We talked, but it wasn't exactly engaging, and then we went to bed ourselves. We slept in the same bed and messed around some, but nothing about it was smooth. In hindsight, nothing was smooth with her ever for the next sixteen years as well. I got up the next morning and thought to myself, *I am never talking to that bitch again*, and I didn't for over a month. Then one day, Roseanne called me with her whiny voice, asking me to call her because we were both going to the upcoming wedding and she didn't want anything to be awkward. Frankly, nothing would have been awkward. I would have just ignored her ass. Anyway, after her call, I was alone at home and didn't have much going on because it was wintertime, so I called her. Next thing I knew, she drove down to my condo. My condo was small but very nice and was in a very nice area. We went to dinner, and I drove her around and showed her where I worked—the whole community, really. Her behavior was completely different when she saw where I lived, what I drove, and where I worked. Hindsight is twenty-twenty, yes, and she knew exactly what she was doing. I remember thinking to myself all the time, *Why does she act so confident?* It wasn't like she was wealthy or very beautiful. My mom actually told me, "Johnathan, you dated so many beautiful girls. Why would you choose that one?" And she was right. Soon I found myself driving two hours to Aldbridge on a school night to spend the night there and get up at 4:30 a.m. to drive back to school. I wouldn't have said then that I truly loved her, but she was putting on a great act to make me like her. And she stood up to me, and no one else had ever done that. Actually, no one in a relationship should have to stand up to the other person if it's really a relationship. At the time, I liked that she would stand up to me, and I also knew that all my friends were getting married, and I thought that that's what I was supposed to do. That year progressed. Dave and Susan got married, which always brings on more conversations with any single person at a wedding. Roseanne was set to graduate in the spring of '99 from with a degree in psychology. For the record, a bachelor's degree in psychology isn't worth the paper it is printed on as far as real-life employment goes. That was true for Roseanne as well. She would later put it to great use in other ways.

We talked on the phone a lot during these months, and I remember the particular conversation that changed everything. She told me she was graduating in the spring and didn't know what she would do after that. She wasn't staying in Aldbridge and would have to move back home to Southeast Ohio. She knew exactly what she was doing, guiding me to say, "Why don't you move to Shadowmont with me?" Sure enough, that is exactly what I did. She would later spin that into me making her move to a place where she didn't know anyone when it suited her purpose. She had to choose between the Greater Shadowmont suburb, which was in one of the most prominent areas of Shadowmont and comparable to any decent place in Ohio, and her hometown, which was in Southeast Ohio—the most impoverished area in all of Ohio.

She was from Knox County, which is in Riverport, Ohio. It is an extremely run-down, old coal-mine/steel-mill town that's known only for putting out great football players years ago—when the coal mines and steel mills were still open and there were fifteen thousand people living in the town. Now the town is filled with homes that are literally falling down when their owners aren't burning them down for insurance money.

At the time, though, I thought it was neat because so many all-American football and basketball stars had come from her town. She had a tendency to act like she was friends with all of them. She had a propensity for doing that with almost everything. She would put just enough truth in a story to draw you in, but the rest would be lies or embellishments. She would tell these stories with such enthusiasm and fake bravado that they would become completely believable. Through the years, she would perfect this craft.

So in the end, she moved in with me. Her dad had moved to West Virginia with his new wife after the death of her mother. Her mother had passed away before I ever met her but had a serious impact on her, or that's how she acted anyway. Understanding everything about her was difficult as she was and probably still is the most dramatic woman on earth.

I remember calling her dad and asking if I could talk to him when we came to visit. Her dad and his wife had a very small three-bedroom, one-bathroom ranch on a hillside, which every home was in this area as the whole area is in a valley. If you build at the bottom of that valley, you will eventually be hit by a flood, so everyone was on a hillside or hilltop. It took me a couple of mornings to get to be alone with him when everyone else was sleeping. So I did what I felt was the right thing to do: I asked him if I could marry his daughter. He, of course, said yes. Not that I was the greatest thing ever, but at this time, I was working five jobs, and that was completely unheard of to people in this area. At this time, I was a teacher, football coach, strength coach, and track coach, and I ran a speed camp in the summer. This area was full of people working off of government assistance, drugs, crime, and illegal schemes. The only people with any real money were involved with the area's half-assed Mafia and gambling machines or were taking advantage of the impoverished people of the towns by renting these shacks to them and having the government pay the rents.

I proposed that evening at a park in West Virginia, and she said yes. We were married that next November in her hometown.

CHAPTER 14

MARRIED LIFE BEGINS

The night before our wedding, as with most weddings, there was a rehearsal dinner. Everyone on both sides is introduced, has dinner, and then goes to the church to practice the ceremony for the next day. For us, everyone met at the hotel bar/restaurant afterward. I had all my old friends from the lake there and some friends that I hadn't seen in years. Roseanne and almost everyone else went back to their rooms by ten. Since my friends had come all that way, I wanted to stay and talk to them. I drank water all night as they got drunk at the bar. It didn't bother me a bit because I wanted to catch up with everyone. I excused myself at around 1:00 a.m. as I obviously had a big day ahead. I drove past the nice hotel and Roseanne's room on my way down the hill to the cheap hotel where I was staying with my parents that night. My mom, dad, and I woke up early and went to breakfast. We showered and were all getting dressed. The phone rang, and I answered it; it was Rosanne. She immediately screamed, "What the fuck were you doing, driving by my motherfucking room at 1:00 a.m.! I told you to go to bed early! Can you do that? *No*—it's only our fucking wedding day!" She said a lot more, but you get the point. It was awful, and five seconds into the barrage, I held the phone away from my ear. My parents' eyes were big, and their mouths were open. I tried in vain to explain what I had done or didn't do; it fell on deaf ears. After I got off the phone, my dad, while tying my tie, said, "It's not too late, Johnathan. It's not too late." This was the best piece of advice that my dad had ever offered me, and I chose not to listen. Her explosion was so bad, I was wondering if she was going to show up. I could have easily just said "You know, I'm not going through with it," and canceled the whole thing. I thought I'd have just been out a couple of grand. I didn't, however, and later, I found out I was out $633,000. Live and learn. Unfortunately, I found out later that this was what she did. She would explode like that over nothing. It was so bad, I didn't want to argue about anything because the effort required was just too much. Could I win every argument? Absolutely. But I would have to almost completely check out to do that, and I had better things to spend my time on. That did happen a handful of times through the fifteen years we were together, and she would cool it for a month or so before going back to her controlling ways.

So we were married in November and went back to Shadowmont. We weren't going to honeymoon until the next summer, so I went back to teaching and coaching. At the time, she had a clinical job where she kept tabs on people with psychological disorders for next to no money. It was as if she never went to college, and I was stuck with paying her student loans too. I was a very naive young man and did not pay enough attention to the most important decision that anyone will ever make in their life. I have heard people say this after the fact, and trust me, it's true. Your choice in spouse is the single most important decision that you will ever make.

I continued to work hard and make good financial moves. The next big thing that happened is my parents came to visit. They were making me crazy, which parents do, and I volunteered to go get everyone donuts. I was standing there, waiting in line, and I saw a small real estate book that was popular in the late '90s and early 2000s.

I started to page through it and saw these giant lots that were for sale in the township of Townsend. Remember, Townsend was your typical subdivision with quarter-acre and sometimes half-acre lots. These lots were two to three acres. A farmer had parceled out his land and created fifteen huge lots to sell.

I went back home with my donuts and this real estate book. I showed this to Roseanne and asked her if she wanted to take a ride. So we drove by where this was and looked at all the lots that were for sale. I was drawn to a 3.12-acre wooded lot that was huge and beautiful. Real estate was booming at the time, so I thought there was no way I would lose even if I bought the lot and just sat on it. I made an offer that very day. The owner gave me a counteroffer, and I agreed to the price and bought it. So now I owned a condo along with this three-acre lot. I came to find out that the lot immediately appraised for $18,000 more than what I paid for it; I had instant equity. I immediately found a builder that would build on a personal lot, and I went to work on building the biggest house I could possibly afford on this lot. I was thinking about resale before we even began. Just like that, we started building, and in the meantime, I put my condo up for sale. I sold the garage and the condo separately to increase our profits, and Roseanne and I moved into an apartment during the construction. I was not at all happy with being married, but I wasn't going to stop doing solid financial decisions because of that. That fall, after our high school season ended, I remember tailgating at a football game with some relatives and friends. After drinking all day and heading to a bar afterward,

I remember talking to one of the relatives over a White Russian. I remember this because it's the only White Russian I ever had in my life. I'm almost exclusively a beer guy. He asked me how our married life was going. I looked him in the eye and said, "I want to divorce her every single day." He thought I was joking, and I said, "I'm not joking. Every single day, I want to leave." Well, this sent a ripple effect through the family, and it definitely got back to Roseanne. Suddenly, Roseanne was pregnant. We were living in an apartment and had no conversations about having a baby. I just finished saying out loud that I wanted to leave, for God's sake. In hindsight, I can say for a fact that she did it on purpose for two reasons: One, she didn't want to lose her meal ticket, and two, she knew the kind of man that I am and I would never leave once a baby was in the picture, or at least it would take something monumentally bad in order for me to leave. She was right in that respect; it was a very well calculated move on her part, but that's what calculating people do. You should have seen all the dramatics that occurred with the pregnancy. Her shaking and crying when I got home, the eight (yes, eight) pregnancy tests—it was like watching Julia Roberts in some dramatic movie or something. Our new house was finished in the spring of 2001, and Amelia arrived that August. I remember all the details of her birth especially because I rehash them every summer during two-a-days to all the coaches at wherever I am coaching. I was up at 4:00 a.m. and standing by the coffeepot in my brand-new kitchen. I heard a shriek from upstairs and went running up. The entire bathroom floor was covered with amniotic fluid; Roseanne's water had burst. I rushed her to the local hospital, and we got her in the maternity ward. They explained to us that she was not very far along and it was going to be a while. I looked at Roseanne and said, "You're in good hands. I might as well go to practice," and I did. They gave me a beeper in case of an emergency, but they were confident that it was going to take some time. I coached that day in August. At the end of the second practice, while we were all huddled up, my beeper went off. I ran out of there immediately and went straight to the hospital. They had induced labor, but it was still going to take some more time. I slept in a chair that was at the foot of the bed all night, and in the early-morning hours, Amelia arrived. She was a seven-pound and two-ounce baby girl and was as healthy as could be. We got everything settled. Roseanne was good, Amelia was good, and it was about 7:00 a.m. I said, "Nothing more I can do here. Might as well go to practice," and I did. I know that some guys these days are into paternity leave and all that. It's just not my nature and not the way I think.

A little over a month later, I was having a PE class, and after it was finished, I went to my office to check my voice mail. (I didn't get a cell phone for years after we got married. Why would I? She would have called me nonstop if I had one. I would question my married friends about having one and compared it to wearing handcuffs.) Roseanne had called me; she said a plane had flown into the

World Trade Center and I needed to get to a TV. I took my entire class upstairs to an audiovisual room where one of the other assistant coaches' rooms was. I had him turn on the TV just when the second plane flew into the second building. It is hard to explain what I was feeling. I know two things: I went home that day while wanting to quit my job and join the marines, and for the first time in my life, I thought it was more important for kids to go home to their families than to practice football. We did practice that day. Our head coach presented it as the Taliban wanting to disrupt our lives and interfere with our country's progress. He had a point, but I still wanted to go home and send our players home. As luck would have it, our stud linebacker broke our starting quarterback's collarbone that day. As Rosanne would say, "Karma!" I wonder if she still says it because in the end, her saying "Karma!" all the time bit her in the ass.

CHAPTER 15

HOME OWNERSHIP

We had just moved into our four-bedroom, two-and-a-half-bathroom brick two-story home when Amelia was born. As it was being constructed, I would drive by there every day after track practice. At one point, there were no walls yet on the second floor, and I remember sitting in what would become a bathroom. I sat on the plywood floor and looked into the woods and was so happy and content. Later, when the house was nearly finished, I went into the house and took a bath in the whirlpool tub just to try it out first. Never in my life had I ever lived in a house that nice, and I was about to own it at thirty years old. We moved in, Amelia was born, and then 9/11 happened. It all happened very quickly. I, of course, was worried about the debts we had—student loans, credit-card debts, and house loans—and of course, against my better judgment, I bought Amelia's mom (who did not have a job now) a brand-new sport utility vehicle because apparently, there was no way she could drive the one mile to Kroger and back safely without doing it in a vehicle such as that. In the end, I would make sacrifices worth hundreds of thousands for that person against my better judgment just because it wasn't worth the argument and unending drama.

The thing I loved the most about living in this first home during those three years was taking care of the yard. I would give Amelia her bath every night. I worked a lot, obviously, and it was some of the only time I got with her when she was a baby. The yard and woods, as I mentioned, were 3.12 acres, but I really enjoyed planting seeds, fertilizing, mowing grass—everything involved with the yard. Plus it gave me an opportunity to get away from Roseanne and drink beer. I bought my first riding mower from one of my players for $100. It was way too small for me and the yard, but it was fine because I was still out there, cutting grass for the previously mentioned reasons. I must have looked funny as I rode that little thing with no shirt on. I didn't care; the tractor, house, and yard were all mine, and that felt really good. I've always pretty much kept the same schedule of going to bed early and getting up at or around four. I have kept that up for the past twenty-five years. My mind has always worked best in the morning and worst in the evening. When you go hard at what you're doing all day, it works that way. I remember looking at Quicken during those years and seeing all the debts we had. I wanted to chip away at those enough to knock them out, but the task seemed to be overwhelming. I remember that Roseanne had about $20,000 in student loans; I had about $16,000 in student loans. She brought with her a number of credit cards that I would juggle back and forth between 0 percent interest offers. After we had been there for three years, I had the house appraised; it was now worth over $140,000 more. Everything in that area was appreciating so fast that I wanted to do it again one more time on a larger scale and then downsize and live debt-free. To me, that is the most comforting feeling in life—not having any financial stress. We had looked at a model home that was huge. It was incredible, and I was young and confident in my ability to flip a house, and at the time, the market was outstanding. We put our house up for sale and put a deposit down to build a 4,800-square-foot home. At the time, the banks were handing out loans like they were candies, and builders were building homes on next to nothing. They broke ground on our new home with a mere $3,000 deposit. These practices would later cost the banks and everyone else and cause the housing market to collapse.

So we owned our original home, and it had not yet been sold, and the second home was nearing completion. Fortunately, I was coaching a kid whose dad was becoming my friend, and he owned a lot of properties that he rented out in the surrounding areas. He turned me on to the idea of doing a lease option to buy on my first home. This is where a tenant gives you cash up front that is nonrefundable unless they ultimately purchase the home. Four different tenants gave me big cash deposits, and I had to evict three of the four. It was a pain in the butt, yes, but in my mind, they gave me thousands of dollars for that pain during the time. Every tenant thinks they are going to purchase the home, but in the end, they can't buy a home, especially during that year for some reason. The fourth one actually managed to purchase the home. At first, this was very stressful because I was about to have a mortgage on my first home and another one on the much-bigger second home. It was over half a million dollars in mortgages on one teacher's salary. I was able to pull it off by showing that the first house was under a lease option to buy a contract; they could treat it like it didn't exist and only concentrate on the second home. No way would a bank do that today, but in those days, I was able to pull it off.

Once we moved into our new home, the plan was to live there for three years, sell it, and downsize. The first home had eaten all the debt we brought into the marriage, so we wanted to make another huge profit and walk away. Three years came and went, and times were tight, but we were making it on me continuing to work my five jobs. We didn't have any bad debt anymore. I had the second house appraised. I paid over $300,000 initially, and it appraised for like $480,000. I immediately put a "For Sale" sign in the yard. The appraisal was the good news; the market collapsing was the unanticipated bad news. Now we were in this home for the long run. In hindsight, it was a calculated risk, and had it paid off, it would have been great. As it were, Amelia had a great place to grow up in. The neighbors and neighborhood were outstanding. The house itself just proved to be cumbersome as it was too much to clean, cost too much to heat and cool, and cost too much in general during that time. Then I made a decision that would alter the course of our lives.

CHAPTER 16

PURCHASING THE TIME-SHARE

The year before, I had a very stressful football season. Between overcoaching our team and going home to a control freak who never complimented anything I did, something finally gave. I ended up in the hospital with blood pressure that was off the chart. I had never had a blood-pressure, cholesterol, or any other kind of health issue before or after this time, so this probably took on the shape of a nervous breakdown. At one point, the doctor stated that if I wasn't in the shape of a professional athlete, I would have had a heart attack. The doctor shut me down for the next six weeks. Basically, I sat around the house and did nothing that was difficult for a guy like me. But I needed to keep my mind and body active. During this downtime, I started asking myself, *When was the last time you had a vacation, John?* The answer was college—during spring break in Florida. In twelve years of teaching, I hadn't gone anywhere to relax. I always wanted to work and never miss a single workout with the team. Over time, that will take a toll on anyone.

That spring, we were at a neighbor's house. They were constantly going on trips to one place or another. I asked them, "How is it that you can go to so many places?" They explained that they were on vacation years before and did a time-share tour. They call you in, give you drinks, and explain how great it would be to own a time-share and travel the world. They ended up purchasing the rights to 69,000 time-share "points" that were to be used throughout the year. They paid $35,000 up front and paid a maintenance fee of $800 per year. They explained that there were weekend-getaway deals and last-minute deals, so the points they had were more than enough because all these deals didn't take away from the points they were allowed with their purchase.

As I explained earlier, during these years, the housing market, bank loans, and economy were all down. That summer, I wasn't busy one day, and I was looking around online. I soon found a time-share with 89,000 points, which was even more than our world-traveling neighbors'. People were getting rid of their time-shares because they didn't want another maintenance bill every year. I was just screwing around and went ahead and bid $1, not thinking I would ever get it. The auction lasted 8 hours, and it was 11:00 a.m. So I didn't think much of it and met some neighbors at the pool, and we were drinking beer and talking for most of the afternoon. I brought up my bid and was immediately getting screamed at, of course, for not asking her permission. She went on and on about maintenance fees—blah, blah, blah. In hindsight, her antics were laughable. She had no job and hadn't had one for years but wanted to dictate where every dollar went. Don't get me wrong—I fully understand the value of a stay-at-home mom. At this point, though, it was clear that this woman had no intention of ever having any kind of gainful employment—child or no child. The party soon went back to my house so we could check on it. Sure enough, I was still winning the auction. Later, we did a countdown, and in the end, what my neighbors had purchased for $35,000, I got for $1. The bottom line for me was that I needed to go on vacation, and I thought it was important for Amelia to experience things. Everything our neighbors said about the time-shares was true. We went on two trips that summer, another the following Christmas, and another on spring break. It didn't cost us much at all to stay at our time-share, so we used the heck out of it for about a year. They offered so many deals that we really didn't have to use our points either. We had a surplus all the time. These were nice places that we were going to too.

It was nice to finally be going on vacation and relaxing. I had definitely overworked myself for years. Things would change for us a couple of years later. At this point, both of Roseanne's parents had passed away, and she had one sister left, Sarah. I hadn't seen Sarah except for a couple of times since our wedding years ago. She had a job, a house, and a boyfriend and had always kept to herself. One day, Roseanne sat me down and explained that Sarah had a rapidly advancing disease and she was no longer able to work; she was losing her home, and her boyfriend could no longer care for her. This was all news to me, and I was pretty shocked. All I remember saying is "If Sarah needs help, let's help her." Soon after that, Sarah moved in with us. We converted a room downstairs into a bedroom for her as it was adjacent to a bathroom. When she moved in, she was walking with a walker. This didn't last long. She was soon scooting to anywhere she needed to go, which usually was the bathroom, her La-Z-Boy chair, or her bed. Needless to say, our lives changed. Roseanne would take care of her meals during the day, and I would give her shots of her medicine in the evenings for some time. This would put a damper on our vacations for years to come because it was like taking care of an adult child.

Because we weren't using our time-share, people started asking if they could use it. These condos would retail for thousands of dollars a week, and we would get them for $500 or less. So Roseanne started renting weeks to our friends for usually around $1,500. This soon turned into a business for Roseanne. Over the next few years, neighborhood friends, gymnastics parents, friends of friends, relatives, and everyone else were going to her for trips. And for a couple of years, it was amazing. People were pulling in the driveway and handing her checks all the time. I'd be cutting the grass and would see three cars with people I had never seen before come and pay her. People would return from vacation and give her bottles of wine, gift cards, thank-you cards, etc. Roseanne and I had budget meetings, and I couldn't believe what she was taking in. I was leaving her notes that instructed her to overpay on everything and believed she was doing it. We were doing well when my car's transmission finally gave out. I felt comfortable with buying a three-year-old Cadillac for myself, and then a month later, I bought one for Roseanne too. In my opinion, I could pay off mine in six months and then Roseanne's in nine months. Then those extra car payments we piled on the house. That's what I was doing on my Quicken program. That's what we discussed in our budget meetings. It was in the notes I would leave for her at 4:30 a.m., and then I'd call her to check if she had done what I asked by midmorning—when she finally woke up.

Roseanne used her sick sister as a crutch constantly. She used going to the bank as a way of getting out of the house for a break from Sarah. She used having a PO box as a way of having extra protection for Sarah—from what, God only knows, but understand that Roseanne was a master manipulator with serious control issues and a degree in psychology. She soon was bringing people in to teach them her business and presented it as an investment opportunity. I didn't ask a lot of questions because it wasn't worth it. I just wanted to teach, coach, drink my beer, and pay off my house. I was happy that she was finally making money, so I didn't argue with her. During these years, as a getaway from Sarah, we started going to a casino in another state. We had always gone to the dog track whenever we went to her hometown. I saw all of this as harmless fun. At the dog track, I would place a $2 bet, get a beer, and watch a race. I would do that for ten races and maybe win one, which would pay for my beer for that night. So when we would go to the casino, I would have $100, and we would both play penny slots. If I was up, I would keep going while drinking beer and talking to people. If I started getting down, I'd go to the bar and watch football. Roseanne would usually sit at the same machine all night long, which was fine with me. She had me believing that she won all the time and always had cash to show me. Understand that I never had an ATM card; I hadn't written a check or gone to the bank for years either. Roseanne had done all of that as a "break from the house." In the end, this was a serious tactical error on my part. God forgive me for actually trusting my wife. So our dates during these years were all spent at the casinos. Then Roseanne started telling me that she would get "free money." The amounts she would tell me were pretty substantial, so I thought she had to play them. She would call me and say things like "I have a free $300. What should I do?" I would say "Go play it." It was a win-win for me. I was under the delusion that she won all the time and I got to be alone and away from her. In the end, the supposed free $300 was really like $30. She was really good at using just enough truth to draw you in and then embellish the story with lies.

I had never been around gambling while growing up, so I didn't see how it could become an addiction. It never crossed my mind that a person could become addicted to it, really. My mindset was always to go for fun, play a little, and hopefully cover that night's beer, gas, and food; that was a good night. If she had developed an alcohol or drug addiction, that would have been a lot more noticeable to me. So this became our life for those few years: She and I would go to the casino one weekend night a week as a date. Roseanne would then go another three nights during the week, and I would pick up Amelia from gymnastics, make dinner, or do whatever. I didn't think much of it and was happy that she was gone. People were still going on trips left and right, and our mortgage was going down like crazy, or so I thought.

CHAPTER 17

THE BEGINNING OF THE END

In January of that year, I felt like we had finally made it. According to my Quicken program, everything was paid off. For any of you who used this program around then, there was a running tab of a person's net worth in the bottom left-hand corner of the screen. It would calculate your assets and compare them to your debts. I remember our net worth being $633,000, and I was a forty-two-year-old teacher and coach. In my opinion, I needed to teach ten more years before I could do whatever I wanted. So when Roseanne presented me with the idea of going on vacation for the month of June, I thought, *No problem*. Roseanne claimed that a woman was willing to rent her island home to us for the month for $700. I was coaching one of the premier high schools in the nation at this point, and we were only required to attend six workouts in the summer, so getting away was not an issue at all for me and wouldn't affect our team. Next thing I knew, we were flying, heading for our vacation. I had $3,000 in my wallet, and Roseanne had another $5,000 in her purse. We rented a car for the month and drove to the three-bedroom, two-bathroom island house, which would be our home for the next thirty days. It was on stilts and had an outdoor shower underneath it and an in-ground pool at the back. It was everything we needed or wanted. My biggest concern with Amelia was her gymnastics. She couldn't miss a whole month of practice and keep up with her teammates. Competitive gymnastics was a year-round sport. Before we left, I made arrangements with a gym in the area so Amelia could continue to practice while we were on vacation. I joined a gym as well so I would have something to do while she was practicing for four hours. During this vacation, my days usually involved just Amelia and me. Roseanne was constantly on her phone, talking to various people about vacations. Four days a week, Amelia would practice. On those days, Amelia and I would go on adventures; we went out to eat, went to the beach, went to the pool, and just did vacation activities during the day. Then in the afternoon, I would drive her to practice. Once I got her settled in there, I would go to my gym and work out. I would then head back, pick up Amelia, and head for the bridge to the island. Every time we went over that bridge, we paid a $6 toll, but I felt it was worth it if it let Amelia keep doing her gymnastics. Then on the days Amelia didn't have gymnastics, I would usually go to the beach and drink beer. I remember that one day, it was raining, and I took a bike and went to a little place so I could sit at a bar and have some beers by myself. I loved it. I just felt free that day.

We had visitors drop in, but really, they were mostly Roseanne's family. Her aunt and uncle lived nearby, and I remember we had a beach day. Roseanne kept leaving the beach and fielding phone calls. The longer we were there, the more her phone kept blowing up. Her aunt commented, "Is it always like this?" I just said, "She always gets calls, but they are coming more and more now." At one point, we flew in Amelia's cousin, who would stay with us for a week. I took him and Amelia on a charter-boat fishing trip for a whole day. We caught all kinds of fish, and the mates filleted all of them for us, and we had a huge fish fry that night. The kids loved it. That whole month was Amelia and me and whomever else. Roseanne was rarely involved with anything but her phone. Toward the end of that month, people were calling and becoming very angry. At this point, she wanted me to talk to some of them. I had no clue about what she was doing or how to do any of her vacation stuff, so her wanting me to talk to anyone didn't make any sense to me. It would be like me having her coach football for me.

We went home in early July, and from that point on, life got really crazy. Roseanne was constantly outside, smoking and talking on the phone. When she wasn't doing those things, she was at the casino. Everything just developed a weird feel. August came, and I was working for twelve hours a day and wasn't around. School started in September, so I was up at 4:00 a.m., left for the gym at 5:00 a.m., taught from 7:30 a.m. to 2:30 p.m., and then coached from 3:30 p.m. to 6:00 p.m. We would watch a film afterward. I was getting home at eight on a normal night, so I didn't even see her every day. She told me that she couldn't pay the electric bill because Social Security had frozen our accounts and I needed to cash in my retirement. I thought, *What the hell? She's being absolutely crazy. There is no way a guy like me would ever do that. It's the worst thing a person can do unless there is absolutely no other option.* She told me she was in trouble—that there'd been a misunderstanding and I needed to pay people off so they didn't sue us. I was stunned. We were now at a point where I was pulling in at night and was seeing people carrying out our dining-room set and the deck furniture we just bought before we went to Sanibel. And then they came for Amelia's bedroom furniture and my bedroom furniture. (Roseanne had slept on a couch in the basement and I had slept in a king-size bed by myself for the last eleven years of our marriage.)

Football season is stressful enough with its very long hours, but it becomes even more so when your furniture is disappearing. Then the police started showing up at the door, asking for Rosanne, and eventually news crews and reporters knocked on our door. Meanwhile, she had led me to believe that we had won some kind of lawsuit for hundreds of thousands of dollars and even showed me a paper that was supposed to be proof of it. I thought that the only way to save her was to resign, cash in my retirement, pay the people she owed, and use the money we won to start over somewhere. I believed that because my house and the cars were paid off and we had won some money, everything would be fine. *I can get a teaching and coaching job somewhere. We can downsize and come out of this OK.* I really thought it was all a huge misunderstanding when I was in the middle of the hurricane. Now I can spot control issues and manipulation from a mile away, but during that time, I was completely blind to all of it. So life was like this from July to January 2014. The furniture was mostly gone, phone calls kept coming, the police were at the door, and I had resigned from my job. I knew that was a mistake before I did it, while I was doing it, and immediately after I did it, but I truly felt like this was the only way to help my wife. Right after I resigned, I drove to the worst dive bar in the world and ordered one pitcher of beer after another until a friend came to get me and take me home. I knew something was very wrong, but I couldn't see clearly in the middle of that hurricane. I didn't like Roseanne, let alone love her, but I felt this sense of obligation to take care of her because that's what I signed up for. Maybe there is such a thing as being too good of a team player, but that was all I had ever known.

CHAPTER 18

AFTER JANUARY 6

I did spend three mornings with my head down on my marble kitchen island, crying as Amelia ate her breakfast. I did promise her that I would always take care of her. I had no idea how I was going to do it, but I knew I would find a way. Those three days, I took Amelia to school and then went to the gym and worked out. On the first day, after I worked out, I informed my family. I had been estranged from my family for most of my marriage. Controlling, manipulative people work to keep you close to them and keep the people who care about you and will help you far away from you. Despite me not seeing them or talking to them much, they all rushed to my house that weekend. On the second day, I was doing damage control on things like my phone. I dropped Amelia off at school, worked out, and then drove to Verizon because my phone was acting strange. Mind you, I thought my bill was paid six months ahead as I did with my insurance and all my other bills. I explained what was happening, and they pulled up my information. The man's eyes went big and said, "Mr. Sizer, you're behind $2,400."

This was just the beginning of these types of conversations, but I definitely would need a phone because I was going to apply for every single job I could think of. I had $1,600, and that was it, so I certainly wasn't going to give this person a penny at that moment. When hit with something like this, your pride suddenly goes away. From college through all my adult life, I had prided myself on paying, overpaying, or paying early all my bills. Something like this happens, and you go into pure-survival mode like a wounded animal in the woods. Fortunately, I was raised like I was. I had experienced having no heat in my home before, and I had experienced living on ramen. The prospect of moving was no big deal to me as I had moved nine times before I was eighteen. All the things I hated while growing up were now providing me with the tools I needed to survive this situation. On the third day, I cried, took Amelia to school, went to the gym, worked out, and then got pissed. I thought, *Fuck this! I'm going to quit feeling sorry for myself and find a job!* I went home and got on the Internet and started applying for everything you could think of. That day, I received an email from an athletic director from Roseanne's hometown; it said that the head coach had just resigned and if I was interested, I had to send a list of references. My Internet and cable at home had already been cut off, along with our heat, so I was doing all of this with my phone. I quickly put down a dozen names and phone numbers on a list and hit Send. It made that jet-airplane noise as it was sent. Two seconds after that, my phone completely died. When people say that everything happens for a reason, they are right. I had to then go to plan B with my phone. I had to think of a way to communicate that was bare-bones cheap. I went to a store and got the cheapest phone with the cheapest plan and paid for one month's service. My contacts were transferred, and I could at least field a call if someone called me for an interview.

After I got my phone situated, I drove to the county courthouse. I wanted to file for a restraining order. They asked me if there had been any violence. I said no. They said, "Well, you can't file for a restraining order, then."

I said, "I need to speak to someone because I'm terrified of what I will do if I ever see Roseanne again."

They put me in front of a magistrate, and I gave a one-hour-long, recorded dissertation of everything I knew that she had done. As soon as I left that place, I did the same thing in the next county with the same police officer who had been at my doorstep many times before, and I lied to him. I wanted to protect myself because I was really afraid of seeing her and losing my temper.

That weekend, my parents, my sister Connie, and her husband all came to the house to be with Amelia and me. We had a family meeting, and no one could believe what had happened. My mom said, "I know these things happen—just not to my son." Connie and her husband were the biggest help through this. Connie immediately took Amelia to get her a phone and put it on her plan. We then talked about what I was doing. I informed everyone that I was applying everywhere and Riverport had already contacted me, and I strongly felt I could get that head-coaching job with my experience and background. Connie put a plan in place. If this did happen, she would give me her minivan because the Cadillacs wouldn't be mine for much longer. Talk about pride going out the window. A week earlier, I wouldn't have been caught dead in a minivan. Connie also said that if this went through, she would handle my moving expenses and get us set up in a place. She told me to try not to worry too much about anything and concentrate on getting a job. On Sunday, Connie and James went back home, and my parents stayed at my house to help out with things. Amelia still had school and gymnastics, so I was getting her to those things and working out by myself in order to keep my sanity. That week, my phone rang, and it was Riverport. They asked me if I could come for an interview. I said, "Absolutely!" and we set it up for the following week. That weekend, Amelia had a gymnastics meet out of town. She rode with her teammates, and I drove there on my own. I was driving when my phone rang. I answered and heard a woman's voice and the wind blowing in the background. The voice on the phone said, "You need to come get me!"

I said, "Who is this?"

Roseanne had the nerve to call me for help! As far as I was concerned, we were completely done on January 6. Apparently, she had conned some of her relatives to bail her out of jail, and now she needed a ride. I proceeded to go on a barrage of profanity with all my suggestions as to how she could find a ride. This was one of the last conversations I ever had with her. In the end, it was me doing all the screaming.

I went to Amelia's meet and was driving home when my mom called me; she was apparently hiding somewhere in my house. She whispered, "Johnathan, you're not going to believe who is here. Roseanne just walked in. I turned around, and she was there. I couldn't believe it. When will you be home?"

The audacity of this woman to show up after all she had done! I got home and met my parents. Roseanne was hiding in one of the thirteen rooms that the house had. I talked to my parents and then went to the basement. Roseanne was sitting in one of the few chairs we still had left and holding Amelia. I sent Amelia upstairs, shook my head while looking at Roseanne, and went up myself. She then came upstairs, and I was in a room all by myself, and she was telling me all the things I needed to do for her the next day: take her to court, talk to her attorney, go get her cigarettes, etc. I just squinted my eyes and said, "I'm never doing anything for you ever again."

She looked at me with the most evil look I've ever seen and said, "You have no idea how vindictive I can be!"

I said "Oh yes I do. Get out of my way" and walked out.

The only funny thing about her showing up and being around those couple of days was the look on her face, which showed how uncomfortable and miserable she was while being around us. At one point, she actually had the nerve to complain about it, wanting it to stop.

For two nights, I slept on the couch with my wallet clutched in my fist all night long. My mom was on my king-size mattress, which was on the floor, and clutching her purse. On the second night, at two in the morning, I had had enough. Roseanne was sleeping on the floor of Amelia's old room: pink walls, random toys on the floor, and no furniture—just a TV on the floor, which was turned on, and a pillow and blanket for Roseanne. I was pissed and marched up the stairs. I opened the door and stood over her, and she woke up, startled. I put my finger right up to her face and said, "Tomorrow morning, I am waking up early and going to the gym to work out. When I come back home, you have your ass in the garage, ready for court. I will take you there and drop you off. When it is over, call me, and I will come get you and take you wherever you want to go, but I don't ever, *ever* want to see your fucking ass after that! Do you underfuckingstand?"

She nodded nervously, and that's just what I did. I got up, worked out, and drove home to Roseanne, who was dressed and ready in the garage. I drove her to the courthouse and dropped her off. After she used her public defendant's phone to call me, I picked her up and said, "Where do you want to go?"

She said, "The casino."

We drove for forty-five minutes without saying a single word. I pulled up in front of the hotel they had and got out. "I'm using the restroom and will be out of here," I told the valet. I used the bathroom and was walking out through the lobby, and I saw Roseanne signing in at the desk. That was the last time I have ever seen her.

CHAPTER 19

RIVERPORT

The next week came, and I had an interview that Tuesday. I knew I needed to do well because this was the only opportunity I had at the moment. I knew the town was less than ideal, but I was going to treat it as the greatest job in the universe. Moving in with my parents and living on government assistance never crossed my mind. My first interview was with the principal, athletic director, and superintendent. The superintendent led the interview, but each of them asked questions. I had quick and very elaborate answers to every question asked and left while feeling very confident that it would lead to a second interview. I had become friends on the phone with one of Sarah's old boyfriends. He was from generations who had lived in this town, and he would end up helping me out quite a bit during the interview process. This level of football and this area of the state were quite foreign to me. His family and I went out to eat after the interview, and then I stayed at his house that night. We stayed up most of the night, talking about football and all kinds of things. He was and is a great guy, and he helped me a lot during this time.

I went back home the next day. Walking into the home I had basically built felt like coming home to an area where a war had just been fought. It was a skeleton of what it once was. This is when I started finding out more and more about the depths Roseanne had gone to cheat people. I got a call from her aunt. Apparently, Roseanne was calling relatives and asking for money, saying it was needed for medication for Sarah. I had given Sarah shots of compaxon for that first year; however, outside of that, she was taking no medication. Her aunt then said that Roseanne had borrowed hundreds of thousands of dollars from her during those years; her retirement was gone, and Roseanne led her to believe that she would be paid back with interest from some lawsuit money she had coming. Roseanne's aunt and uncle gave her thousands of dollars for some mythical medication. Sarah's best friend gave her thousands of dollars for the same reason. These were, by far, her worst crimes; however, these relatives would not turn her in to the police. This would be the equivalent of a parent shaving a child's head just to claim the child had an illness to get donation money so they could go blow it on something else. The thought of this just disgusts me.

I also had close friends coming to the door during this time, telling me she had borrowed $3,000 here and $10,000 there. They would always say she would tell them, "Don't tell John! Have you ever seen John when he's mad?" They would also say, "Do you know how many times I was just going to tell you?" But they never did until after the truth came out. I remember that at this time—adding up the $205,000 she got from my retirement, the $240,000 she took from her aunt's retirement, $40,000 here, $18,000 there, and all the vacations—the grand total was well over $600,000. It was the exact amount that I believed our net worth was. It was all the money she conned and stole from some of our best friends and every single member of her family who had any kind of money. She lied to, cheated, and stole from just about everyone we knew and was only sentenced to a handful of years in prison and was out in less. Had her family pressed charges, I don't know if she would have ever gotten out.

I was granted a second interview and was excited to have the opportunity. It was good for me to get my mind off all that had happened. Football has always been able to guide me in the right direction, and in teaching, when you're older and well educated, sometimes it's the only thing that will get your foot in the door.

My second and third interviews went really well but were dramatically different from the first. The first interview was more about football and situations involving leadership with regard to football. The second interview was with the superintendent, principal, and athletic director; however, most of the questions were about my ex-wife, daughter, what I needed from them, etc. Understand that this was Roseanne's hometown and its people had heard all about it. I'm sure that many people assumed I was involved with what she had done. In this second interview, they asked very personal questions, which I didn't have to answer. Really, they technically had no right, but answering them didn't bother me a bit because I had nothing to hide and I needed a job. I answered everything they asked and left while feeling like I was going to get the job. I went to a basketball game with Joey and met some of the kids and parents. The principal later told me that he thought I was politicking, which was laughable because I don't really even know what that is. I'm not political; I just wanted to see what the kids were like and watch a ball game. I again drove back across the state, went home to Shadowmont, and waited. My phone rang two days later, and it was the superintendent. He said, "How would you like to be the next head coach of Riverport?"

I said, "I would like that. When can I start?"

He set up a start day in early February and said I'd finish out that school year as a substitute but have full benefits. I made a point of saying that right now, Amelia was flying without a net—meaning she didn't have any health-care coverage, and she was still competing in gymnastics. It was now very important to me to keep Amelia's schedule as normal as possible. Let's face it—she's a young girl whose life just completely changed, and her mom had disappeared. I made arrangements with Nancy, the mother of one of her gymnastics teammates, so she could stay with her family until the end of the competition season. Nancy has been a wonderful friend, a mom to Amelia, and just an outstanding person who would drop everything at the drop of a hat to help Amelia these last six years. So Amelia moved in with them for the next two months, and I moved into the upstairs section of a friend's house. I traded my Cadillac to my sister for her minivan. My brother-in-law got to drive it around for a while and really liked driving it around. One day, I got a voice mail from James; it said, "Johnathan, they got the Caddy, man! Shit's getting real, man! They came and took the Caddy!" For him, that's when it really became real.

So I moved into my new upstairs home and was living out of a suitcase. I showed up for my first day at school and reported to the superintendent's office. I thought the hay was in the barn with the position; however, I found myself in front of the school board, being grilled with questions for two hours. This interview was all about Roseanne. The question that stood out to me the most was "It's August 26, and we're getting ready to kick off for our first game. If the sheriff pulls up and wants to arrest you, what do we do then?"

I said, "In order for me to be arrested, I would have had to have done something wrong." I then said, "Through all of this, I was never once questioned, asked for, called in, subpoenaed—nothing. I was never even looked at funny by anyone in law enforcement—not a single time."

I know I was believable because I was never more certain about anything in my life. The school board was then OK with me for the moment, and the superintendent walked me to the high school.

CHAPTER 20

BECOMING A HEAD FOOTBALL COACH

During our walk from the board office to the high school, the superintendent filled me in on all kinds of small-town politics; apparently, there was a qualified hometown guy in the building who was not given the job and I was to beware of him. I really didn't care about any of that. I was going to do what I have always done and care about the kids. The adults never concerned me before, and they wouldn't now. I went to the school and met with the principal. He immediately warned me that some people were not going to be very friendly with me. This all sounded extremely bizarre to me; however, over the next two years, a lot of things would seem very bizarre. Don't get me wrong—I met a lot of outstanding people and families in my two years in this town. Many people cared so much for the school and football program; that part was excellent. They just definitely had a different type of mentality in and around there. As the principal stated, when I was going around to meet people, some would be very excited to meet me, and others would literally look straight to the ceiling and roll their eyes or turn completely around and walk the other way without saying a word. I would literally laugh out loud at this, for I had never ever seen anything like it. Where I was from, people were not like that.

Thus began the hardest two years I have ever worked in my entire life. They had me running in school detention at the junior high, which was nice because that was the best building in the school and had the best quality of people. I would then go after school to run the weight program. When I first saw the kids, I thought they literally looked like whipped dogs. From what I was told, the previous coach would say and do things that were absolutely unspeakable in Shadowmont or anywhere else. He was a hometown hero, so they let it go. I, of course, was an outsider, so I went under the microscope. My biggest point of emphasis was to meet all the kids, get them working out, and help them develop a positive attitude. Football is a fun game, and you should have fun while doing it. So I got up early, worked out at a local gym, and went to school. I trained the team after school and worked on public-relation-type things, like get T-shirts to all the players, local business people, administrators, etc. In fact, driving down the highway next to the river while going to pick up those T-shirts is the last time I have ever spoken to Roseanne. She called me and asked who I was associating with in town—as if it was any of her damn business! Anyway, I asked Roseanne why she wanted to know. She said I needed to be careful and watch out for people in that area and this and that. I immediately exploded and screamed, "You're giving me motherfucking advice now?" I hung up the phone and never spoke to her ever again. Ten seconds later, I walked inside the T-shirt place with a big smile and asked how everyone was doing. In this particular area of the state, being the head coach at Riverport is like being some kind of half-assed celebrity. The year before, my high school team was playing on ESPN; this was no big deal. The local TV station wanted to interview me at the field house. I walked in with the athletic director and saw three cases of chili in cans that were stacked on the file cabinet as soon as we walked in. I said, "What is that?"

She said, "Don't worry about it. We will throw that away."

I did my interview and left. Keep in mind that my $1,600 was nearly gone. I was driving my sister's minivan. My sister had given me a credit card for my living expenses, which I would have to eventually pay back. I was paying rent by having my sister pay the cable and electric bills where I stayed during those two months. Those cases of chili looked pretty damn good to me, and if they were just throwing them away, what the hell? I went down there that night and threw them in the van and took them home. I lived on that for a while. I kept the last can for the longest time to remind me of this time. I also kept the last dollar of the $1,600 in the ashtray of the van for the longest time also.

The first two months flew by, and now it was time for Amelia and me to get our own place. A businessman in town was nice enough to allow us to move into a house that he owned, and I only had to pay the mortgage, which was less than $500 per month. Relative to where we came from, this was literally a shack—a two-bedroom, one-bathroom shack. Its porch was falling off the front, and it had no extras at all. Just envision something you would see on *Hatfields & McCoys*; it wasn't far off from that.

Once Amelia arrived, I wanted her to get on a schedule that was as close to what she was accustomed to as possible. I found a gymnastics gym that was comparable to the one where we used to live that was about an hour away. I had no business with having her continue gymnastics because it cost $500 per month, but I thought it was important, especially during that time, because she was good at it and it would keep her mind off the move and give her a sense of normalcy. In hindsight, I'm very glad that I did it, but my days were brutal during this two-year stretch of being a first-time single dad.

That first football season, my schedule was like this:

4:00 a.m.	Wake up
5:00 a.m.	Gym
6:30 a.m.	School
7:00 a.m.	Put Amelia on the bus
7:30 a.m. to 3:00 p.m.	Teach
3:30 p.m. to 6:00 p.m.	Practice
	(Amelia would be dropped off at the stadium, and my equipment man would take her to carpool.
6:15 p.m.	Drive home and put chicken and vegetables in the Crock-Pot.
6:30 p.m.	Drive to Washington, Pennsylvania
9:00 p.m.	Dinner
10:00 p.m.	Bed

And then I would start it all over the next day. Gymnastics competitions were held in the spring, so I was able to go to all of those. They were happening all over and in different states. Our schedule was like that, and I had to deal with doing things that I was not used to doing. I discovered that I had forgotten how to use a debit card. I had to think before writing a check, and paying bills was foreign to me. At the same time I was dealing with this backward town. I would get sewer bills in the mail for 76 cents. I would think, *Why in the hell are you wasting postage on a bill for 76 cents?* It was mind-boggling.

And listen to this: When I first got to town, they told me I would be a substitute but still have full benefits. I assumed that it would be a first-year teacher's salary or something awful but livable. I was working my butt off, and after the first two weeks, I got the first check; it was $250. My jaw nearly hit the floor. I wanted to throw my suitcase in the back of the van and leave. I wouldn't get paid like a real teacher until September. I had to live off my sister's credit card from February through August. Even when I started getting a full salary, it was $30,000 less than what I had made in the past.

Regardless, sometimes you do what you have to do. Through it all, Amelia and I grew a lot closer. Our relationship completely changed once her mom was out of the picture. Amelia and I were now working like a team. I'm not saying that it was or is perfect; she still has a tendency to talk to me like she's my wife, and I have to put her in her place from time to time.

I coached there for two seasons, and I'll spare you all the details. The bottom line is that we were 3–7 and then 2–8. I went there with a continuing contract, and if they had me back for a third season, they would have had to grant me a continuing contract there too. I was an outsider and not worth the risk. That combined with a new superintendent and principal was not a good combination. When I was let go—I'm not going to lie—I was extremely insulted, but in the end, they did me a huge, huge favor! It was hard to see when I was going through it, but it is super obvious now. When you're fired for the first time in your life and especially by people like that, it is an insult. I had to drive near there not long ago, and I couldn't believe I had actually lived there. We did live there, and we did survive it. It made Amelia and me much stronger. The timing was also good as she was finishing eighth grade. I was determined to have her attend one high school after my experience of attending four.

CHAPTER 21

MOVING BACK TO THE LAKE

Once I realized I was not going back to Riverport, I applied to every single head-coaching opening in Ohio. I had some interviews and a couple of second interviews. I seemed to come in second often. I had two choices in my mind: Move to Aldbridge, live with my sister, and try to find something, or move back to the lake and make it work. I moved back to the lake and Sandtown. I had no job and no prospects. My plan was to apply for every football job around and try to get on at a school. Amelia and I moved into a furnished lakefront condo. We had to get a furnished one because when we left Riverport, I sold every single piece of furniture I owned as I didn't want a single memory of my marriage. I was really rolling the dice because I knew I would be paid through the summer but had no job for sure on the horizon. I knew I needed to network and get my name around, so that's what I did, but this would be another challenging year. There were two high schools in town, and one had pole vault and diving, and the other school did not. I felt that Amelia's gymnastics background would help her move forward in these events. There are no gymnastics gyms here at all, so we transitioned her to school sports after the move. The next thing I did was look for a football job. I found one at a small local school, and they worked to help me find a teaching job as much as they could. Then at the end of August, I found a PE job at a charter school in a nearby city. This was an experience because charter schools are extremely underpaid, the kids behave terribly, and it is run like a business and not a school. For example, during my first week of teaching, a fifth-grade boy started throwing repeated punches at a girl's face while holding her hair at the same time. I pulled him off her and walked him to the office with my arm around his shoulder. The principal came in five minutes later, and I assumed she would want to hear my version. She asked me if I touched him. I said, "Of course I did. He was hurting her." I got in trouble for touching him, and he was back in class the next day. Every student had a dollar sign on their head, and they worked to keep them in school no matter what kind of poor behavior they exhibited.

That winter and spring, I took a track-coaching job at a school that was an hour away from where I lived and twenty-five minutes from where I worked. I was just trying to network until I could put it all together. I had coached against this school in the past, so I knew other coaches there. So I coached football at one school, taught in a second school, and coached track in a third—all while driving in this giant loop and making even less than what I did at Riverport. This particular year, I started doing CrossFit in the mornings to keep my sanity. Don't get me wrong—Amelia and I loved living on the lake, but there was no way I would teach a second year at that charter school. I had to find something that would fit us and get us back on track. I found myself complaining about teaching every day, and that wasn't like me at all. I would finish doing CrossFit and be walking into our complex while thinking to myself, *Something has to give for us here.* I felt like I was doing all the right things to get myself out there.

That spring, while looking online, I saw an ad that said that Coldhall High School needed a defensive coordinator and linebacker coach. This was right in my wheelhouse, so I called the school. The head coach had coached for a few years in the big city I had previously lived in and knew of the school where I had coached. He wanted me to meet him immediately. I was very thankful because he advocated hard to get me in there. Coldhall is a smaller version of what I was used to. The high school is beautiful, the workout facilities are excellent, I was very well paid, and it's full of good people. They wanted me to coach football badly but didn't have a teaching opening. Right then, Sandtown had me in for an interview also, and they were going back and forth between them. Just then, Coldhall had an intervention-specialist opening, and I discovered I could work under a supplemental license for three years while I completed all the coursework and passed the praxis tests to become certified. I had five separate interviews at Coldhall—head coach, athletic director, principal, superintendent, and finally, the director of special education. I was finally offered the job! I was so thankful to be in a school with good kids and a calm environment, teaching with people with intelligence, and driving to one place every day. It had been a lot of work; I had to take six special-education classes during this time. I had to pass a special-education praxis exam and a foundations-of-reading praxis exam in order to finally become certified as an intervention specialist. I did all of that while learning how to write IEPs. Taking classes and passing tests in a subject area outside your expertise after not taking a class for seventeen years is very, very difficult, but I was able to do it. Now I have my certification and a continuing contract at Coldhall schools. I no longer need to stress, and I'm thankful for that. Most importantly, Amelia is now a senior in high school. In her four years here in Sandtown, she has lettered in cross-country, swimming, diving, and track. She is a National Honor Society officer and a member of the student council, Aim4Excellence, Move 2 Stand, and the bio clubs at her high school. She has been named the Student of the Month by the Elks Club, the Lions Club, and the Ohio Lottery. She has five different jobs that she rotates throughout every season. Frankly, she has turned out to be just an all-around outstanding kid. She has written papers and has never once used what happened with her mom as an excuse to give up or quit.

Amelia will be attending the Academy of Shadowmont in the fall of 2020 and will be majoring in special education. She wants to become a special-education teacher, coach, and club adviser. Thank you, God, for giving me the strength to get her through high school.

Printed in the United States
By Bookmasters